Metamorphose eines Warenhauses
Metamorphosis of a Department Store

Metamorphose eines Warenhauses
Metamorphosis of a Department Store

Ingenhoven & Ingenhoven

Prestel   München · Berlin · London · New York

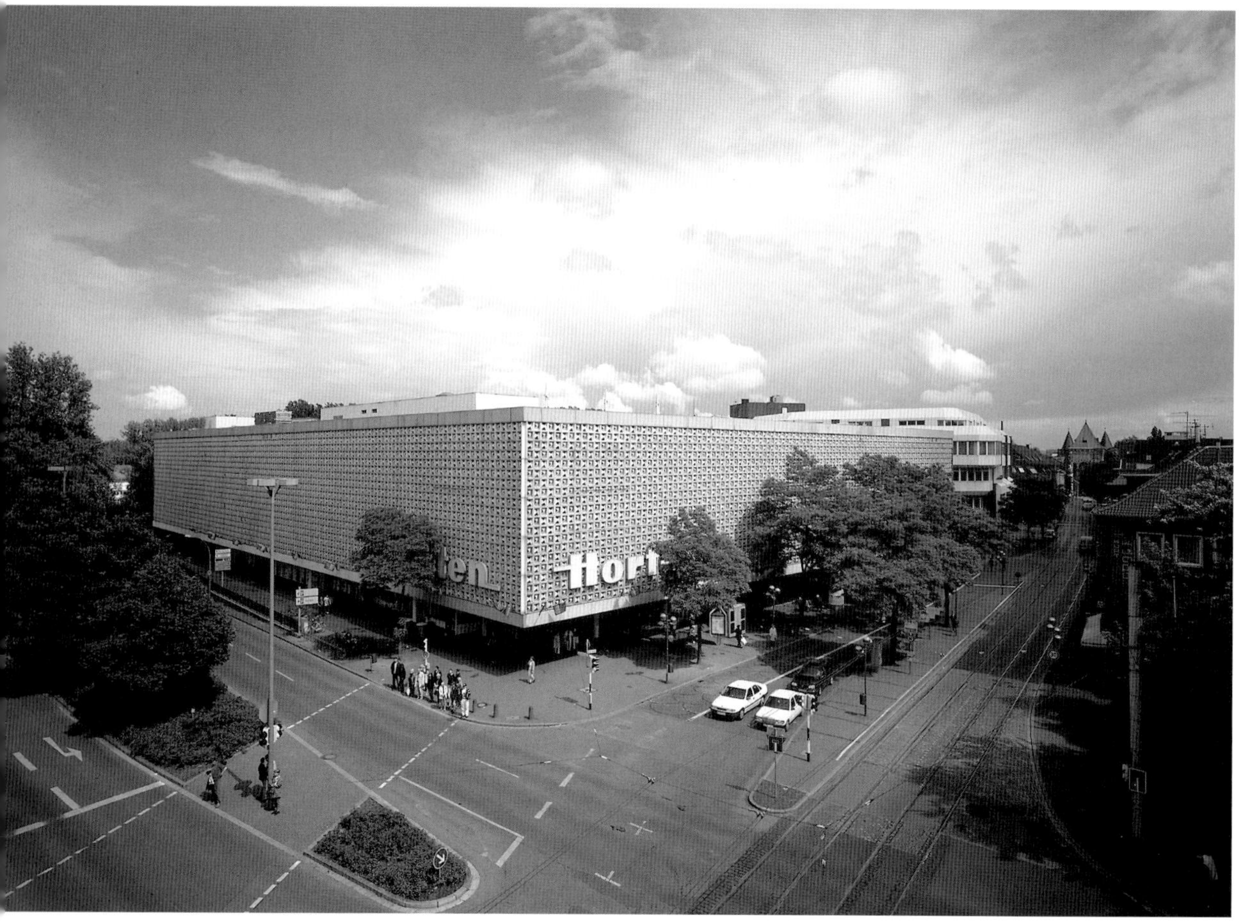
ten
Hort

Olaf Winkler

Horten Stadt Neuss
Horten City Neuss

Eine Aura des Aufbruchs umgab den Fremdkörper, der in das Gefüge der niederrheinischen Stadt einbrach: Von Modernität, mehr noch, vom »modernsten Warenhaus Westdeutschlands« war die Rede, als das Merkur-Kaufhaus 1962 in der Neusser Innenstadt eröffnete. Tatsächlich war damit beides gemeint, sowohl State of the Art als auch Zugehörigkeit zur architektonischen Moderne. Letztere hatte sich vom Vorkriegsideal der herrlichen Körper im Licht entfernt, propagierte zunehmend autogerechte Trassen im urbanen Umfeld und dazwischen zweckdienliche Quader im Gewand einer neuen, industriellen Epoche. Für den einstigen Typus des Kaufpalastes bedeutete diese Art Funktionalismus generell die Wiederannäherung an den Lagerhausgedanken und das Bereitstellen weiter, ungeteilter Flächen, auf denen sich die Waren dem Kunden wenig geordnet in den Weg legten. Die räumliche Struktur verflachte zum einfachen Stapel; Glaskuppeln und Lichthöfe waren passé und ließen die Kleinteiligkeit reichgegliederter und großzügig durchbrochener Fassaden, wie sie die Jahrhundertwende noch gekannt hatte, gleich mitverschwinden. Was sich im Rückblick als Irrweg einer gesamten Typologie darstellen mag, hatte Konzept: Die Tiefe der Räume verlangte künstliche Beleuchtung, Mischlicht aber galt für die Präsentation der farbigen Waren als nicht mehr dienlich. So emanzipierten sich die Bauten von der Sonne und von der Stadt.

Das Besondere der Merkur- und späteren Horten-Warenhäuser wie in Neuss lag nicht in der Problematik – die sich vom Trend nicht unterschied –, sondern in der konkreten und in Deutschland bis dahin beispiellosen Antwort darauf. Die Gitterwerkfassade, von Helmut Rhode erstmalig für Duisburg (1958) konzipiert und von Egon Eiermann in ihre schließlich populärste Form aus Keramikelementen überführt, bedeutete in ihrer Vereinheitlichung die Erfindung

The alien object that thrust itself upon the urban fabric of Neuss, a town on the Lower Rhine, had an aura of something entirely new. When the Merkur department store opened in 1962 in the centre of the town, there was talk of "modernism" – no, more than that – of "the most modern department store in West Germany", by which two aspects were implied: its state-of-the-art design and its sense of identity with the Modern Movement. By that time, of course, Modern Movement architecture had departed from the pre-war ideal of the body beautiful bathed in light and had increasingly come to propagate efficient highway systems intersecting the urban environment and interspersed with functional blocks – all in the spirit of a new, industrial age. Compared with the historical building type of the palatial department store, this form of functionalism implied a general reorientation towards an emporium-type concept with the creation of broad, undivided areas in which the many wares were distributed in the path of customers in more or less random order. The spatial structure was reduced to a simple stacking of storeys. Glazed domes and atria were passé, and the small-scale structure of richly articulated and perforated facades that were common at the turn of the 19th and 20th centuries disappeared at the same time. What in retrospect might be seen as a wrong line of development for a whole building type did have a certain logic, though: the great depth of the internal spaces necessitated artificial lighting; and since mixed forms of lighting were regarded as unsuitable for the presentation of coloured products, buildings of this kind emancipated themselves from the sunlight and the city outside.

The remarkable aspect about redeveloping the Merkur and later the Horten department stores, like the one in Neuss, lay not in overcoming problems of this kind, which were a common phenomenon anyway, but in the actual solutions found for them –

Verwaister Koloss: So nachdrücklich, wie sich die Horten-Bauten als ortlose Ikonen der City-Entwicklung etablierten, sträuben sie sich gegen Verwandlung und Umnutzung. Das Neusser Warenhaus, an der Kreuzung zweier zentraler Verkehrsadern gelegen, schloss 1999 seine Pforten.

Abandoned colossus: just as emphatically as the Horten buildings established themselves as icons of urban development that were not specific to any location, so they now resist conversion to new uses. Situated at the intersection of two main traffic routes, the store in Neuss closed its doors in 1999.

eines baulich umgesetzten Corporate Identity-Prinzips. Dieses konnte unabhängig von den Architekten der einzelnen Projekte, die folgten, Bestand haben; der Neusser Baukörper etwa wurde von Hentrich + Petschnigg Architekten, Düsseldorf, (Architekt: Hans Köllges) entworfen. Die gleiche Fassade macht es heute so leicht, ein Horten-Haus zu demontieren: Nimmt man ihm die Haut, ist es seiner Bedeutung nach getilgt; was bleibt, ist ein Koloss, den der Verlust der Maskerade endgültig unansehnlich werden lässt. Umso mehr offenbart sich in diesem Moment, dass die eigentliche Leistung des Konzepts über die Erfindung eines originären Dekorsystems hinausging. Diese Hülle bemühte sich nicht einmal um Vermittlung zur Stadt, sondern schnitt den Körper aus dem urbanen Raumgeflecht heraus – und verlieh ihm damit eine neue, fast unerwartete städtische Funktion. Die monofunktionalen Kisten im ubiquitären Gewand gerieten im Einzelnen zu Landmarken, an denen man sich in den Cities der sechziger Jahre orientieren konnte.

Horten Neuss
Fast unmöglich scheint es, in die Reste eines solchen Warenhauses neuen Sinn hineinzutragen, es sei denn, man ließe es wieder bei einer ähnlichen Funktion bewenden, wie es etwa bei Umbauten in Hamburg oder Aachen geschehen ist. Dennoch ist in Neuss die Ausnahme gelungen; und der dortige Umbau ist angesichts seiner Position im Stadtgrundriss explizit vor dem Hintergrund städtischer Fragen zu lesen. Das Haus steht am Südende der Haupteinkaufsstraße in Sichtweite geschichtsträchtiger Orte wie Rathaus oder Quirinusmünster und am Beginn der Kulturachse, die etwa die Stadthalle, das Clemens-Sels-Museum und das zur mittelalterlichen Stadtumwallung zählende Obertor verbindet. Impulse für die Neugestaltung des obsolet gewordenen Busbahnhofs gegenüber, für den

solutions that were unprecedented in Germany at that time. With its uniform, standardized appearance, the openwork facade, first conceived by Helmut Rhode in 1958 for a project in Duisburg and later developed by Egon Eiermann into its most popular form – a facade clad with ceramic elements – heralded the principle of corporate identity in building. The style could be maintained in successive projects for which different architects were responsible. The building in Neuss, for example, was designed by Hentrich + Petschnigg Architects, Düsseldorf (project architect: Hans Köllges). The facade is also what makes it so easy to dismantle a Horten store today. If one removes the skin, the significance of the building is eradicated. All that remains is a colossus, rendered unsightly by the removal of its mask, which shows that there was more to the concept than the invention of an original decorative system. The skin did not even seek to relate to its urban environs. On the contrary, it served to carve the volume from the surrounding urban fabric, thereby lending it a new, almost unexpected urban function. In the 1960s, these ubiquitous monofunctional boxes with their uniform attire became landmarks and points of orientation in our cities.

Horten, Neuss
It might seem almost impossible to invest new significance in the remains of such a department store, unless one were to settle for a similar function again, as has been the case in Hamburg and Aachen, for example. In Neuss, however, a successful exception has been achieved. In view of the location of the complex within the urban topography, the conversion should be seen explicitly in the context of the overall urban planning. The complex is situated at the southern end of the main shopping street in sight of historical buildings like the town hall and the Minster of St Quirinus and at one end of the cultural axis that

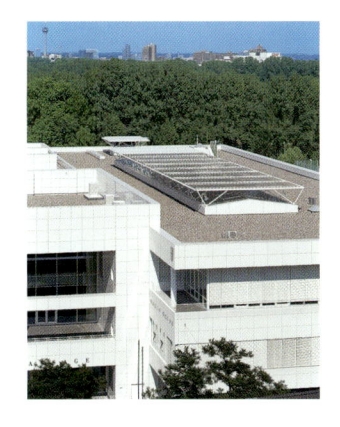

schon ein städtebaulicher Wettbewerb durchgeführt wurde, sowie des Hafenareals im Norden können von hier ausgehen; das Viertel selbst, seit Schließung des Horten-Hauses ohne ausreichenden Einzelhandel, bedarf neuer Perspektiven. An diesem neuralgischen Punkt künftiger Zentrumsentwicklung haben die Neusser Architekten Robert und Oliver Ingenhoven das im Februar 1999 geschlossene Kaufhaus in nur 21 Monaten Bauzeit zum kompakten städtischen Ensemble gewandelt. Dieses beherbergt nun den Sitz der Kreisverwaltung, den neuen Spielort des Rheinischen Landestheaters (RLT), ein Programmkino, Gastronomie und eine Ladenpassage. Das RLT, die Hälfte der Spielzeit als Wanderbühne in der Region unterwegs, hat nach rund 40 Jahren provisorischer Einrichtung in einem ehemaligen Biergarten eine angemessene Heimat gefunden; der Kreis erhält die Gelegenheit, seine in Neuss verteilten Ämter 25 Jahre nach der kommunalen Neuordnung zentral zusammenzuziehen und den Hauptsitz der Kreisverwaltung von Grevenbroich in die Kreisstadt herüber zu holen. So vereint das Projekt nicht nur kulturelle, politische und kommerzielle Funktionen unter einem identitätsstiftenden Dach, sondern führt auch private Hand, Kommune, Kreis und Region partnerschaftlich zusammen.

Vollzogen wurde die Metamorphose mit Hilfe radikaler architektonischer Eingriffe, die vom ursprünglichen Erscheinungsbild des Baukörpers kaum mehr etwas ahnen lassen. Strahlend weiß öffnet sich eine rationalen Gesetzen folgende Bauskulptur der Stadt und den Besuchern; sie ist Ergebnis eines Prozesses, den die Architekten untertreibend als »Subtraktion alles Nichtbrauchbaren« umschreiben: Nicht viel mehr als das Stahlbetonskelett mit seinen Achsmaßen von 9,50 x 10,60 Metern und ein Großteil der Deckenfelder blieben vom Bestand erhalten, und selbst dort wurde eingegriffen. Eine halbe Achs-

links the civic hall, the Clemens Sels Museum and the Obertor, one of the gateways in the medieval city walls. Ideally, this new development should provide impulses for the redesign of the obsolete bus station opposite it, for which an urban planning competition has already been held, as well as for the harbour area to the north. New perspectives are also required for the neighbourhood as a whole, which has been without adequate retail amenities since the closing of the Horten store. At this critical node of future developments in the town centre, the Neuss architects Robert and Oliver Ingenhoven have transformed the department store, which closed its doors in February 1999, into a compact urban ensemble – in a construction period lasting only 21 months. The new complex now houses the district administration, the new stage of the Rheinisches Landestheater (RLT), an arts cinema, gastronomic facilities and a shopping arcade. After 40 years in provisional accommodation on the site of a former beer garden, the RLT, which tours the region for half the season, has at last found a fitting home. Similarly, the district administration, which has been scattered about the town since a local government reform 25 years ago, now has the opportunity of bringing together all its departments in a single location, as well as transferring its headquarters from Grevenbroich to Neuss. The project thus unites cultural, political and commercial functions beneath a single roof. Here, too, private enterprise, municipal, district and regional government enter into a new partnership.

The metamorphosis was achieved by means of radical architectural measures that leave virtually no trace of the original appearance of the building. This gleaming white built sculpture is based on rational laws and opens itself up to the city and the public. It is the outcome of a process the architects describe, with a certain understatement, as "the subtraction of everything super-

Annäherung an eine neue Epoche: Die Architekten verwandelten das immense Volumen des einst feindseligen Quaders in eine gegliederte, aufgebrochene Struktur, die sich nun freundlich und bewegt der City zuwendet. Die Formensprache zeigt Züge der Internationalen Moderne der Vorkriegszeit.

The dawning of a new age: the architects transformed the huge volume of this inimical cubic block into a well-articulated structure that addresses the town in a friendly, lively manner. Its formal language reveals features of the International Style of the pre-war period.

länge des statischen Grundgerüsts wurde entfernt und hinten wieder angefügt, eine ansehnliche Rundung als Antlitz zur Stadt formuliert. Lange Fensterbänder, kleinere Vor- und Rücksprünge und das in Teilen freigelegte Stützensystem unter einer gerasterten Leichtmetallhaut rhythmisieren nun die Fassade. Der Anklang an Entwürfe Richard Meiers ist nicht unbedingt gewollt, doch über die gemeinsamen Vorbilder begründet. Wie bei den reinweißen Bauten des Amerikaners bezieht sich die neu gefundene Formensprache in Neuss auf die internationale Moderne der Vorkriegszeit. Sie führt über die sechziger Jahre hinweg zurück in jene Epoche, in der der fließende Raum nicht an den Rändern des Baukörpers ausgegrenzt wurde.

Der Wandel zum Organismus
Den prägenden Impuls gab dem architektonischen Konzept jener Eingriff, der die große Form verändert und sie damit dem neuen gestalterischen Willen unterordnet. Die Architekten teilen das Gebäude entlang seiner Mittelachse in zwei gegeneinander verschobene Hälften und setzen den einst fast abstrakt anmutenden Quader in Bewegung. Mit der Verabschiedung von der äußeren Primärform wird der Übergang zum auch ästhetisch wirksamen Organismus geleistet, der es erlaubt, differenziert auf die neuen Anforderungen von Funktion und Repräsentation zu reagieren. Die Teilung entspricht der Zuordnung der beiden Hauptnutzungen im Komplex; sie erhalten eine gewisse Eigenständigkeit, ohne die Einheit des hybriden Gesamtsystems aufzugeben. Tatsächlich besitzt die neu eingeführte Grenze auch rechtliche Bedeutung, denn die Bauherrenschaft teilen sich der Kreis Neuss und der Neusser Bauverein; letzterer hat darüber hinaus die Koordination des Gesamtprojekts übernommen. In die von der City abgewandte Hälfte ist die Kreisverwaltung mit den Büros für 265 Mit-

fluous". Virtually the only elements to be retained were the existing reinforced concrete skeleton frame, with axial dimensions of 9.50 x 10.60 m, and large parts of the floor bays; and even here, changes were made. Half the length of one bay of the structural framework was removed at the front and added on at the rear. In addition, a bold curve was created on the side facing the city. The facade is now rhythmically articulated by long strips of fenestration, small projections and recesses, and the partially exposed column grid behind the lightweight-metal cladding. The echoes of designs by Richard Meier are not necessarily intended, but were probably inspired by common models. Like the pure white buildings by the American architect, the new formal language in Neuss harks back, via the 1960s, to the International Style of the pre-war period, to an age when the sense of flowing space did not terminate at the edges of a building.

Transformation into an organism
The decision to change the overall form and subordinate it to a new design goal was fundamental to the architectural concept. The architects divided the building along its central axis into two halves and offset them to each other, thereby creating a sense of movement in what was formerly an almost abstract cubic structure. In abandoning the primary outer form, they have managed to transform the building into an aesthetically effective organism that allows a variety of responses to new functional and formal-representative requirements. The division of the structure also reflects the two main functions it fulfils. The two parts thus acquire a certain independence, without the unity of the hybrid overall system being lost. The newly drawn boundary does, in fact, have a legal significance; for the district of Neuss and the Neusser Bauverein (Neuss Building Association) were joint clients, and the latter was also responsible for coordinating

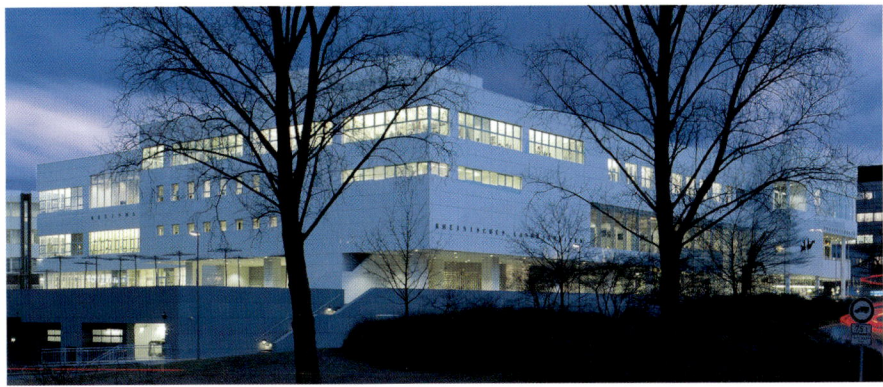

arbeiter eingezogen, vorn, begleitet von jeweils eigenständigem kleinen Programmkino und Restaurant, das Theater. Die Trennlinie zwischen derart sortiertem Kultur- und Ämterangebot markiert im Erdgeschoss – formal der Theaterhälfte zugehörig – die neue, 70 Meter lange Passage mit 12 Ladenlokalen und zugeordnetem Lebensmittelmarkt im Untergeschoss. Das während der vorausgegangenen öffentlichen Diskussion zunächst als 3-Säulen-, mit Hinzukommen des Kinos schließlich als 4-Säulen-Modell bezeichnete Konzept hat eine in der Außendarstellung wie in der inneren Gewichtung logische Struktur erhalten.

Sowohl der unterschiedlichen Funktion als auch ihrer Positionierung entsprechend, unterscheiden sich dabei die beiden Hauptbauteile ihrem Charakter nach. Der Verwaltungstrakt ist hartkantig geschnitten und wirkt geschlossener. Grundlage für die Orientierung eher nach Innen waren insbesondere die konstruktiven Bedingungen; die bauliche Tiefe des Bestands führte zu einem Belichtungsproblem, das die Architekten mit Hilfe eines zentralen Lichthofs lösten. Vom separaten Eingang des neuen Kreishauses an der Oberstraße reicht der Hof als einfach geformter, die gesamte Höhe des Gebäudes einnehmender Frei- und Erschließungsraum unter Glas weit in den Baukörper hinein. Treppen und Aufzüge, zum Teil wieder in die vorhandenen statisch wirksamen Kerne eingepasst, sind von hier aus zugänglich. Der neuen Belichtungssituation folgend, wurden die Büros im Süden zweibündig in den sich ergebenden Trakt einsortiert, entlang der gebäudeinternen Trennlinie einbündig; ›vor Kopf‹ befinden sich Säle und ein mit einem eigenen Oberlicht versehener Konferenzraum im oberen, zweiten Geschoss. In seiner Anlage entspricht der Verwaltungstrakt damit – separate Struktur innerhalb eines größeren Systems – der Typologie von Bürobauten um eine große Halle;

the overall project. The district administration, with offices for 265 local government employees, occupies the tract facing away from the town centre. At the front is the theatre, together with a small independent arts cinema and a restaurant. On the ground floor, the division between the various arts facilities and the local government offices is formed by a new, 70-metre-long arcade, which, formally speaking, belongs to the theatre tract. The arcade contains 12 shops and affords access to a food market in the basement. Initially, during the preliminary phase of public discussion, a concept based on three functions was foreseen. Later, with the addition of the cinema, this was extended to a four-part model. In terms of its outward appearance and inner balance, this concept has a logical structure.

The two sections of the complex are contrasted in character, reflecting their different functions and their location. The clean-cut volume of the administrative tract has a somewhat closed appearance. Its more introverted character is mainly the outcome of structural constraints. The depth of the existing building posed a lighting problem which the architects resolved by incorporating a central atrium. This simply shaped glass-covered courtyard and circulation space extends from the entrance to the new district administration offices in Oberstrasse into the depth of the structure, and rises over its full height. From the atrium, there is access to the staircases and lifts, which in part have been fitted into the structurally efficient existing core. In response to the new lighting situation that was created, the offices are laid out in a two-bay form in the southern tract and in a single-bay layout along the internal dividing line. At the ends are halls and a second-floor conference room with its own roof light. The administrative tract is an independent unit within the overall system and corresponds to an office development type laid out about a large hall. As a result of the "inherited"

Die scharf geschnittenen rückwärtigen Fassaden halten die Form des einstigen Kaufhauses in Erinnerung. Gleichzeitig reflektieren sie funktionale und stadträumliche Bedingungen: die größere Introvertiertheit des Kreishauses und die ›Abbruchkante‹ der Innenstadt Richtung Europadamm und einstige Rheinauen.

While the sharply drawn lines of the rear facades are a reminder of the form of the previous department store, they also reflect the present functional and urban-spatial conditions: the introverted nature of the district administration tract and the "cut-off" face of the inner city in the direction of the Europadamm and the former Rhine meadows.

das konstruktive ›Erbe‹ hat den Räumen derweil eine sonst kaum denkbare lichte Höhe von bis zu 3,50 Meter eingebracht.

Der ›Kulturtrakt‹ nimmt demgegenüber eine extrovertiertere Haltung ein, die sich – nicht zuletzt durch die dem Gesamtensemble als Erkennungszeichen dienende Rundung – am öffentlichen Stadtraum orientiert. Geleitet von der zurückspringenden, ebenfalls geschwungenen Verglasung gelangt der Besucher, von der Stadtseite oder vom rückwärtig gelegenen Parkhaus kommend, in das Erdgeschoss mit Garderobenfoyer und Abendkasse. Von dort führt eine simpel erscheinende, aber in ihrer Positionierung wohl begründete Treppe hinauf zur eigentlichen Theaterebene. Auf halbem Weg hinauf wendet sich die Laufrichtung, der Blick öffnet sich durch die Panoramascheiben in Richtung des Quirinusmünsters und des der Neuordnung harrenden Busbahnhofsgeländes. Großzügig inszeniert, setzt sich dieses Blickwechselspiel mit der Stadt im weiten Foyer fort und findet in der zur Oberstraße vorgelagerten, zehn Meter hohen Loggia seinen Schlusspunkt. Im strengen Kontrast dazu verbirgt sich der steil ansteigende Theatersaal für 450 Zuschauer gleichsam im Innern des Bauwerks; er wurde als intime Blackbox konzipiert, die durch helle Birkenholzsegel unter der Decke akzentuiert wird. Insgesamt erstreckt sich das Theater mit allen Bühnenbereichen, Neben- und Büroräumen über fünf Ebenen. Eine Studiobühne im Untergeschoss dient als zusätzlicher Spielort, ebenso kann das Foyer für Veranstaltungen genutzt werden. Das Restaurant, das im Erd- und im ersten Obergeschoss die Flächen hinter der geschwungenen Fassade belegt, versorgt das Theater gastronomisch. Darüber kam als letztes Element, bereits nach Beginn der Umbauarbeiten, das ›Hitch‹-Programmkino mit 83 Sitzplätzen hinzu, das auf diese Weise einen Lichtspielsaal mit raumhohen Fenstern erhielt. Während der in

structure, the rooms have a clear height of up to 3.50 m, which would be scarcely conceivable under other circumstances.

The "arts tract", in contrast, has an extroverted nature and addresses the urban space – not least in the form of the curved front that functions as an emblematic feature of the ensemble as a whole. Following the line of the set-back glazed facade, which is also curved, visitors approaching from the town centre or from the parking block to the rear enter the building at ground floor level, where the cloakroom foyer and box office are situated. From here, a seemingly simple yet well-judged staircase leads up to the actual theatre level. Half way up, the staircase changes direction and a panorama window opens up a view in the direction of St Quirinus and the bus station area, which still awaits reorganization. Staged on a grand scale, the reciprocal visual links with the city are continued in the foyer and terminate in the 10-metre-high loggia-like structure that faces on to Oberstrasse. In strict contrast to this, the steeply raking lines of the theatre auditorium, with seating for an audience of 450, are concealed within the building. The theatre was conceived as an intimate "black box", the interior of which is articulated by light-coloured birch sails suspended beneath the ceiling. The theatre tract, including all stage areas, offices and ancillary spaces, extends over five levels. A studio stage in the basement provides an additional venue. Similarly, the foyer can also be used for various events. The restaurant on the ground and first floors behind the curved facade also serves the needs of theatergoers. Forming a crowning element above this is the "Hitch" cinema with 83 seats. Added after the conversion work had started, the film theatre has an auditorium with room-height windows. If the staircase inserted into the existing core does not seem entirely appropriate for public use, the apparent contradiction of a cinema with large windows proves to be a genuine

Die Erfindung der dynamisch gerundeten Ecke bildet den konzeptionellen und räumlichen Ausgangspunkt des neuen Organismus. Form und Funktion – die unteren beiden Geschosse der Rundung beherbergen ein Restaurant – verbinden sich zur empfangenden Geste.

The idea of the dynamically rounded corner was the conceptual and spatial genesis of the new organism. The lower two floors in the curved section of the building house a restaurant, so that form and function are united in a welcoming gesture.

einen bestehenden Kern eingefügte Treppenaufgang auf eine öffentliche Nutzung wenig vorbereitet scheint, hat sich der vermeintliche Widerspruch im Saal als Glücksfall erwiesen. Wenn die Vorhänge erst vor dem Hauptfilm geschlossen werden, trägt das Kino auf seine Weise zur Attraktion im Stadtraum bei.

Einpassungen: Im Innern

Die qualitätvolle Einpassung insbesondere der ausgreifenden Volumina des Theaters in das vorgefundene System stellte eine der besonderen Anforderungen dar. Bereits mit der Manipulation an der stadtseitigen Gebäudeecke wurde dem statisch wirksamen Skelett seine Rolle zugewiesen: nicht als unverrückbare Physis, sondern als Regelwerk, das für die weitere entwerferische Arbeit den notwendigen Grad an Freiheit bereithält. Die Konsequenz daraus waren jedoch nicht rücksichtslose Eingriffe; schließlich mussten lediglich zweieinhalb Pfeiler weichen, um den Zuschauerraum als ungebrochene Form und allen Anforderungen eines modernen Sprechtheaters gemäß auszubilden. In der Halle des Kreishauses ebenso wie im Theaterfoyer und in der Loggia durchschneidet das orthogonale Tragwerk den Luftraum; die Träger und Stützen werden nicht als deplazierter baulicher Rest wahrgenommen, sondern als Ordnungssystem, als cartesianisches Prinzip. Es öffnet die Räume, statt sie zu verengen, und stellt zwischen den beiden Bauteilen des Komplexes ein Kontinuum her, das gleichzeitig Unterschiede verdeutlicht. Der Lichthof des Kreishauses betont in seiner schlanken, hohen Ausformung die strenge Fügung und serielle Reihung der Träger – ein Eindruck, den die Beschriftung mit den acht Namen der im Kreis Neuss versammelten Städte bzw. Gemeinden unterstützt; im Theaterfoyer scheint der Raum frei zu fließen, sich vom Regelwerk ausgehend zu entfalten.

stroke of luck. Since the curtains are drawn only shortly before the screening of the main film, the cinema makes its own contribution to the attractions of the urban space.

Accommodation of internal structures

Accommodating the great volume of the theatre into the existing system posed a special design challenge. With the modification of the corner of the building facing the town centre, the role of the structurally effective skeleton frame had already been defined: not as an immovable physical entity, but as a system with sufficient flexibility to allow an ongoing process of design. Nevertheless, the architects did not implement a series of measures that ignored the existing structure. In the end, only two and a half piers had to be removed to accommodate the auditorium in an uninterrupted form and in compliance with the needs of modern stage drama. The orthogonal load-bearing structure intersects the theatre foyer, the loggia and the hall of the district government offices. This three-dimensional grid of beams and columns is not perceived as an intrusive remnant of the former building, though. It forms an ordering system, a kind of Cartesian principle, opening up the spaces instead of constricting them. It also establishes a continuum between the two parts of the complex, a continuum that at the same time reveals the differences between them. The tall, narrow shape of the atrium in the administrative tract accentuates the strict, serial order of the rows of beams – an impression heightened by the lettering they bear: the names of the eight towns and communities that make up the district of Neuss. In contrast, the freely flowing space of the theatre foyer appears to evolve from the order of the structural grid.

Here one finds a further reference to modernism – in this case, to the modernism of the post-war period, when great importance was attached to the theatre, notwithstanding the pre-

Vor- und Rücksprünge des Gebäudes leiten den Besucher in die neue Tranktor-Passage und hindurch zur rückwärtigen Terrasse. Die raumhohe Verglasung der Ladenlokale lässt sich vollständig öffnen und mildert so die Linearität des 70 Meter langen Weges.

The projections and recesses in the face of the building usher visitors into the new Tranktor Arcade, which leads through the building to the terrace at the rear. The full-height glazing to the shop fronts can be completely opened, which helps to relieve the linearity of the 70-metre-long route.

Der erneute Anklang an die Moderne – in diesem Fall der Nachkriegszeit, in der man dem Theater gegen alle wirtschaftlichen Zwänge hohe identitätsstiftende Bedeutung zusprach –, hängt mit dieser Haltung zusammen: Trotz der unerwarteten Weite wirkt das Foyer nicht verschwenderisch; die gestalterische Rationalität erinnert an die in den fünfziger Jahren mit sparsamen Mitteln, aber in klarer Formensprache errichteten Theaterbauten in Gelsenkirchen, Münster oder auch im benachbarten Mönchengladbach, wo eben jetzt der entsprechende Bau kommerziell ausgerichteten Planungen zum Opfer fallen soll. Ingenhoven & Ingenhoven orientieren sich an den damaligen zurückhaltenden, von Gradlinigkeit bestimmten Raumkompositionen; die Materialpalette reduziert sich auf wenige Stoffe wie Putz, Birkenholz, Glas, Leichtmetall. Das langgestreckte, tiefblaue Gemälde, das der Berliner Künstler Salomé für das Foyer anfertigte, fügt sich – obwohl in der Länge zu unentschieden – fries-ähnlich in diese Architektur ein.

Einpassungen: Im urbanen Kontext
Das Prinzip der Einpassung wiederholt sich im Großen. Entstanden ist ein Ort, der die neu eingetragenen Funktionen und die dafür gefundene Gestalt als Teil des urbanen Ganzen definiert; das (Wohn-)Viertel selbst, zu dessen Nahversorgung der Komplex nun wieder beitragen kann, rückt an die Stadt heran und erhält die Chance, eine seiner city-nahen Lage entsprechende Bedeutung zu erlangen. Schlüssel zum Entwurf war auch aus dieser Perspektive die Öffnung der geschlossenen Form, sowie die Gestaltung und Neudefinition der angrenzenden Flächen. Vorhandene räumliche ›Kräfte‹ und stadthistorische Komponenten übernehmen dabei jene Funktion eines Regelwerks, die im Innern das statische System besitzt. So wird das vorhandene Untergeschoss für die Gesamtfigur als Sockel verstan-

vailing economic constraints. Despite its surprising extent, the foyer does not appear spatially profligate. The rational quality of the design is reminiscent of the clear formal language of the theatres erected with limited financial means in the 1950s in Gelsenkirchen, Münster and the nearby town of Mönchengladbach, the last of which is due to be sacrificed to a new commercial development. Ingenhoven & Ingenhoven's design echoes the restrained, rectilinear spatial composition typical of that period and uses a restricted range of materials such as plaster, birch wood, glass and aluminium. The long, dark-blue painting created by the Berlin artist Salomé for the foyer accommodates itself to the architecture like a frieze, although it is perhaps too indeterminate in its length.

Accommodation to the urban context
The principle of accommodation to existing circumstances is repeated at the macroscopic scale. The location created here defines the newly introduced functions and the form that houses them within the overall urban fabric. The new complex makes a genuine contribution to the local amenities of this (residential) neighbourhood, with the result that the area is drawn into a closer relationship with the town and can attain the significance its proximity to the centre would lead one to expect. In the light of this, opening up the sealed volume of the former building was also a key aspect of the design, as was the planning and redefinition of the adjacent areas. Existing spatial "forces" and historical urban elements function as a regulating system in much the same way as the structural system does internally. The existing basement can thus be interpreted as a plinth on which the entire building stands. At the rear, on the side facing the former Rhine meadows, the plinth structure emerges from the ground, tracing the historical line of the town walls, which continues to the north on the other side of the Am Kehlturm road. The architects'

den, der hinten, zur ehemaligen Rheinaue, sichtbar wird. Dort zeichnet er den historischen Verlauf der Stadtmauer nach, der sich im Norden jenseits der Straße Am Kehlturm fortsetzt. Parallel zu dieser Linie könnte nach dem Wunsch der Architekten künftig eine Fußgängerbrücke hinüber zum Gelände des Busbahnhofs und Richtung Hafen die Einflechtung in den Stadtgrundriss weiter festigen. Über dem Untergeschoss wurde, auch in Vorwegnahme dieser Planungen, eine baumbestandene Terrasse ausgebildet, die die Fläche erstmals dem öffentlich nutzbaren Raum zuschlägt und Blicke über die schwer zu zügelnde Verkehrsschneise Europadamm hinweg auf den Neusser Nachbau des Shakespeare'schen Globe Theaters und die Galopprennbahn erlaubt.

Dem Baukörper mit seinen Perforierungen gelingt es währenddessen, die achsiale Dynamik der aus der City herführenden Haupteinkaufsstraße aufzufangen und sie in verschiedene Richtungen aufzufächern. Ähnlich selbstverständlich wie in das Theater gelangt man, von der tief gestaffelten Fassade geleitet, in die Passage und über die Terrasse zum zeitgleich mit dem Umbau renovierten Parkhaus auf der Rückseite. Das Gebäude öffnet sich, nimmt den Besucher auf und führt ihn weiter, und es bedient sich dabei nicht einmal neuer Wege: Die Linie, die die Ladenpassage nachzeichnet, führte schon zuvor als ›Trampelpfad‹ im städtischen Geflecht durch die Verkaufsflächen des Horten-Hauses zu jenem Parkhaus (einst das erste seiner Art in Neuss); nun wurde sie zur innenliegenden Straße transformiert. Gestalterisch stellt diese Traverse leider die Problemzone des Projekts dar; an dieser Stelle erweist sich die überlieferte Raumhöhe als zu gering für die Länge der Strecke, und weder die formal unmotivierte Aufweitung in Wegmitte noch die verglasten, vollständig zu öffnenden Ladenfronten können die Einbußen an räumlicher

proposals for a pedestrian bridge parallel to this line may also be implemented. The bridge would lead across to the bus station area and in the direction of the harbour and would serve to integrate the development even more tightly into the urban fabric. In anticipation of these planning measures, a tree-lined terrace was created on top of the basement, making this area accessible for the first time as a public space and opening up views across the Europadamm – a main thoroughfare that is difficult to contain – to the town's reconstruction of Shakespeare's Globe Theatre and to the horse-racing track.

The volume of the building with its various openings succeeds in absorbing the axial dynamics of the main shopping street from the town centre and fanning them out in various directions. Just as easily as one finds one's way into the theatre, so the deeply set-back line of the facade leads inevitably into the arcade and, via the terrace, to the rear parking block – in those days, the first of its kind to be erected in Neuss – which has been refurbished parallel to the conversion of the main structure. The building opens out, draws in visitors and leads them on, without even having to create a new route: the line followed by the shopping arcade was formerly a well-beaten trail through the sales areas of the Horten store to the parking block. Now this route has been transformed into an internal street, the design of which is problematic, unfortunately. The height imposed here by existing conditions is too low in relation to the length of the arcade, and neither its formally unmotivated broadening in the middle nor the fully openable glazed shop fronts can make up for this deficiency in spatial quality. The fact that the shops within the complex are still finding it difficult to assert themselves indicates that some initiative is needed from the direction of the town centre, which has yet to recognize the challenge posed by this project. A vital measure in this respect would

Kontrastreiche Insignien eines modernen Theaterbaus ohne modische Aperçus: Die lichte äußere Gestalt setzt sich über die Treppe mit Blick auf das Quirinusmünster und im Luftraum des Foyers fort, während der Saal als intime Blackbox ausgebildet wurde. Auf einen Orchestergraben konnte im reinen Sprechtheater verzichtet werden.

Boldy contrasted insignia of a modern theatre without fashionable aperçus. The lucidity of the outer design is continued internally in the staircase – which affords a view to the St Quirinus Minster – and in the lofty foyer space. The theatre auditorium, in contrast, is designed as an intimate "black box". In a theatre created purely for the spoken word, it was possible to do without an orchestra pit.

Qualität ausgleichen. Dass sich die Läden im Komplex bisher noch schwer tun, verweist derweil darauf, dass sich die Innenstadt durch das Projekt, nun im Gegenzug, durchaus gefordert sehen muss. Dazu zählt die Notwendigkeit, eine qualitätvolle Einzelhandelsstruktur generell zu sichern und möglichst bruchlos an das neue Ensemble mit seinen allein kaum lebensfähigen kleinen Geschäften heranzuführen, um die Einbindung auch von Stadtseite aus zu gewährleisten.

Kontinuität und Widerspruch

Unabhängig von diesen Schwierigkeiten verdeutlicht das Aufgreifen des ›Trampelpfades‹ exemplarisch den Umgang mit dem Vorgefundenen. Es mag zumal dem Zugereisten schwerfallen, hinter dem völlig gewandelten Gebäude noch den Vorgänger zu erahnen, und dennoch ist dies auch der Bedeutung nach ein Umbau, kein Neubau. Nur meint ›Kontinuität‹ hier Verbindungen, die sich kaum auf den Oberflächen abbilden. Mit einer Entwurfshaltung, die das Bestehende eher auf Regelsysteme, denn auf erhaltenswerte Bauteile überprüft, gelang es, vorrangig immaterielle Aspekte zu bewahren, die die Gewöhnung und Identifizierbarkeit für den Neusser Bürger ausmachen mögen. Dazu gehören neben jener Wegelinie und den historischen Umrissen des Sockels auch die grundsätzliche (Wieder-)Erkennbarkeit des Gebäudes als markante Einheit und seine Fähigkeit, im Anschluss an den linearen Verkehrsfluss der Geschäftsstraße einen vorläufigen Endpunkt zu setzen. Trotz der räumlichen Verflechtung steht der weiße Baukörper erneut im bewussten gestalterischen Kontrast zu seiner Umgebung; er hat, obwohl zum Ensemble gewandelt, vom einstigen Solitär den Charakterzug des ›Besonderen‹ übernommen. So lässt er sich als ortsstiftendes Element im Stadtbild identifizieren und in die Vorstellung, die man sich von

be to consolidate the qualitative overall retail trading structure and to extend this from the town centre to link up seamlessly with the new ensemble and its shops, which are scarcely viable on their own.

Continuity and contrast

Regardless of these problems, however, the incorporation of an established route through the complex is a good example of the way existing elements have been handled. For strangers to Neuss, it might be difficult to imagine the predecessor of this completely transformed structure behind the present facade. Yet by definition as well as in its significance, this is a conversion, not a new building. Continuity, in this context, means creating links that are scarcely evident on the surface. With a design approach that regarded the existing building as an ordering system rather than a series of elements worthy of conservation, it was possible to retain especially those immaterial aspects of the complex in which the sense of familiarity and identity of the citizens of Neuss is rooted. In addition to the route mentioned above and the historical lines followed by the plinth, these immaterial aspects include a general (re)cognition of the building as a striking unity and the role it plays in marking the end of the linear flow of traffic along the shopping street. In spite of its spatial integration into the urban fabric, the design of this white volume again forms a striking and deliberate contrast to its surroundings. Even though it has now been transformed into an ensemble, the new building assumes the character of a special object like its free-standing predecessor. It lends the urban fabric a sense of place and can be absorbed into the image people have of their own town – both in the present and as a potential source of impulses for future developments. In the way they perform these roles, the "two" buildings – that dating from 1962 and that from 2000 – bear a resemblance to

der eigenen Stadt macht, integrieren – in der Gegenwart und als möglicher Impulsgeber für künftige Entwicklungen. In der Erfüllung dieser Rollen gleichen sich die ›beiden‹ Gebäude, jenes von 1962 und jenes aus dem Jahre 2000, auch wenn sie ihren Aufgaben auf vollkommen unterschiedliche Weise nachkommen.

Die dünnen Fäden, die Alt und Neu verbinden, reißen nicht, weil doch konkret Bauliches mitträgt: Obwohl mit dem statischen System gerade jener Teil bewahrt wurde, der einst kaum in Erscheinung trat, lässt sich dessen existenzielle Bedeutung vermitteln. Erst die Verknüpfung der beiden Kategorien, einer abstrakten und einer konstruktiven Kontinuität, hat es erlaubt, auf der typologischen Ebene radikal einzugreifen und ein Gebilde zu schaffen, dessen architektonische Haltung hinsichtlich Raumbildung, Proportionen, körperlicher Durchdringung sich grundsätzlich geändert hat. Die Haut des Altbaus war nicht perforierbar; sie schnitt wie mit dem Messer ein Volumen aus der Stadt heraus, das im Innern jenseits der Geschosseinteilung praktisch nicht gegliedert, im Äußeren ohne Anschlussmöglichkeit war. Es schuf Gegensätze, und die Grenzhaut entsprach dem Bild, das man sich davon machte. Konträr dazu besteht der neue Zustand im Sich-Öffnen und in der Differenzierung. Das Bild ist nicht mehr zweidimensional, weil verschiedene Orte innerhalb des einen parallel identifizierbar sind. Diskussionen, ob die in schwarzen Lettern auf das Gebäude geschriebenen Funktionsbenennungen überflüssig sind oder ob sie umgekehrt darauf hinweisen, dass der Komplex selbst seine Inhalte nicht zu repräsentieren vermag, gehen am Punkt vorbei. Die Architektur repräsentiert die Zusammenkunft der Nutzer auf einer übergeordneten Ebene, die Schriften die konkreten Bestandteile. Nur wenn letzteres wirklich notwendig gewesen wäre, hätte die Architektur ein Problem.

each other, even if they fulfil their functions in completely different ways.

The fine threads linking old and new are not severed, since the built substance provides support. In retaining the structural system, an element was preserved that was scarcely evident in the previous building. Nevertheless one senses its existential significance. Only by linking the two categories – abstract and structural continuity – was it possible to make a radical intervention at the typological level and create a form whose architectural manner could be fundamentally changed in respect of spatial definition, proportions and volumetric interpenetration. It would have been inconceivable to form openings in the outer skin of the former building. It sheared through the urban fabric like a knife, carving out its own discrete form. Internally, apart from the storey divisions, there was virtually no articulation; and externally, there was no scope for continuation. The building evoked a principle of opposition, and the overall image, determined by the enclosing skin, was an expression of this principle. The new complex, in contrast, is open and richly varied in form. The impression it creates is no longer two-dimensional, since various locations within it can be identified parallel to each other. The whole debate about describing the internal functions in the form of the black lettering on the outside (whether it is superfluous, or whether it is an indication that the building is unable to signify its own contents) misses the point. The architecture signifies the coming together of users on a superordinate level; whereas the lettering denotes the actual elements it comprises. Only if the latter were really necessary, would there be a problem with the architecture.

Urban reconstruction
It was no easy task to coordinate and unite those functions that contribute to the specific character of a town or city. The two main partners in the

Ein zweiter kleinerer Eingang erschließt das Kreishaus auch von der rückwärtigen Terrasse. Im Inneren schufen die Architekten durch großzügige Entkernung eine zentrale Halle, die sich unter einem Glasdach mit außenliegendem Sonnenschutz den Charakter eines im Sonnenlicht südlich anmutenden, nur im Winter leicht temperierten Außenraums bewahrt.

Access to the district administration building is also provided from the rear terrace via a second, smaller entrance. The architects gutted part of the interior to create a central atrium. With its glazed roof and external sunshading, this hall has the character of an external space somewhere in the south, bathed in sunlight and lightly heated only in winter.

Stadt umbauen

Die Zusammenführung stadtprägender Funktionen geschah nicht ohne Schwierigkeiten. Tatsächlich hatten die beiden wichtigsten Partner, das Landestheater und die Kreisverwaltung, längst Anspruch auf selbständige, der kulturellen bzw. politischen Bedeutung scheinbar angemessenere Bauten erhoben; für ein neues Kreishaus existierten realisierungsfähige Pläne für ein Grundstück unweit des heutigen Standorts an der Oberstraße. Ungewöhnlich genug, stammte die Idee für einen verbindenden Organismus von den Architekten selbst. Robert und Oliver Ingenhoven entwickelten, als im Sommer 1997 von einer bevorstehenden Schließung des Horten-Hauses die Rede war, auf eigene Faust erste Pläne. Dass sich die Idee gegen Alternativplanungen – Abriss, Überbauung mit Wohnnutzung – durchsetzen konnte, ist einer langen öffentlichen Diskussion und der Überzeugungskraft des Konzepts zu verdanken.

Die heutige Erscheinung des Gebäudes ist auch im übertragenen Sinne zu verstehen. Der Körper öffnet sich und lässt den umgebenden Raum einfließen, reagiert auf ihn mit Vor- und Rücksprüngen; gleichermaßen aber hat er Fragen der jüngsten Stadtplanung in Neuss aufgesogen. Er beantwortet sie oder führt sie auf ihre Substanz zurück. Erstes gilt offensichtlich für das Theater und das Kreishaus, zwei lange Zeit gärende und getrennt betrachtete Projekte, die nun mit einem Handgriff gelöst wurden; das zweite für die großräumigere Entwicklung des Viertels, der City und des angrenzenden Hafenbereichs. Die neue Figur macht für die Entwicklung in allen drei Maßstäben Vorschläge, die in einfachster Fassung bedeuten: Der Block jenseits der Straße Am Kehlturm ist nicht als Anhängsel an die Innenstadt, sondern als in sich lebensfähige Struktur zu begreifen, die nun weiterer Modellierung bedarf; gerade daraus und nicht

development, the state theatre and the district administration, had long laid claim to their own distinct buildings that would lend clear expression to their cultural and political significance. Realizable plans existed for new district offices on a site not far from the present location in Oberstrasse. Surprisingly perhaps, the idea for an organism that would unite these various functions came from the architects themselves. In the summer of 1997, when word of the impending closure of the Horten department store went round, Robert and Oliver Ingenhoven drew up preliminary plans on their own initiative. The fact that their idea was able to assert itself in the face of alternative plans for demolition and a development of the site for housing purposes may be attributed to the protracted public debate that took place and to the convincing quality of the concept itself.

The present appearance of the building should also be understood metaphorically. The volume opens up and allows the surrounding space to flow in. It responds to the public space in the form of projecting and set-back planes. At the same time, it has incorporated many of the themes contained in the latest urban planning proposals for Neuss, either reacting to them or reducing them to their basic substance. The former approach evidently applies to the new theatre and the district administration, which were fermenting for a long time as two separate projects and which have now been resolved at a single stroke. The latter approach may be seen in the broader treatment of the immediate neighbourhood, the town centre and the adjoining harbour area. The new proposals cover the development at all three scales. Reduced to their simplest form, these can be described as follows. The block on the far side of Am Kehlturm should not be regarded as an appendage of the town centre, but as an independently viable structure that simply requires further shaping. Only in this way, not through isolated measures, can the

aus einem singulären Eingriff kann die Kraft erwachsen, die Haupteinkaufsstraße lebendig auf einen neuen städtischen Schwerpunkt im Süden fortzuführen; und schließlich verlangt all dies nun umso mehr nach längst erhofften tragfähigen Konzepten für den teil-verwaisten Hafen im Nordosten. Das Projekt selbst bedarf, nicht zuletzt zur wirtschaftlichen Stabilisierung des beteiligten Einzelhandels, dieser konsequenten Weiterplanungen, um die angestrebte Einflechtung in die Stadt wirklich zu vollziehen.

Das Ergebnis dieses Projekts ist ein produktives, vielleicht typisch ›niederrheinisches‹ Miteinander, auch in Abgrenzung zum großen Nachbarn Düsseldorf: Neuss bindet über das Theater die Region, über die Verwaltung den Kreis ein – und unterstreicht somit seine eigene Stellung innerhalb der beiden größeren Maßstäbe. Gleichzeitig profitiert die Stadt als historisches Gefüge von der Bekräftigung nuancierter Raumbildungen und Wegeführungen, ganz zu schweigen von der Neuschaffung eines zentralen Theaterbaus in einer Zeit, in der eher Schließungen entsprechender Einrichtungen an der Tagesordnung sind. Und es zeigt sich, dass sich auch sensible Verbindungen innerhalb eines städtischen Wandels mitzuteilen scheinen: Auch – nicht nur – das Horten-Haus steckt noch im Gebäude. Der Umbau in Neuss ist im Generellen vorbildhaft, weil er es im Konkreten nicht sein kann: Trotz jener Zahl an Warenhäusern andernorts, die auch nach der ersten Umnutzungswelle noch nicht ernsthaft ein zweites Leben begonnen haben, lässt sich eine Wiederkehr der hiesigen Situation nicht imaginieren. Das Projekt lebt vom präzisen Umgang mit den Bedürfnissen vor Ort und von einer glücklichen städtebaulichen und stadtfunktionalen Zusammenkunft, die nun von der Stadtplanung weitere Konsequenzen verlangt.

necessary forces be generated that would allow the main shopping street to be extended in a dynamic form to create a new urban focus to the south. Finally, all this calls for long-awaited, functional concepts for the partially derelict harbour area to the north-east. If only to ensure a reasonable degree of economic stability for the retail trade in the new development, a consistent process of further planning is required along these lines to achieve a genuine integration of the amenities into the urban fabric.

The outcome of this project is an example of a productive co-existence that is perhaps typical of the Lower Rhine region, even in the way the scheme demarcates the district centre from its bigger neighbour Düsseldorf. Neuss draws the broader region together through the theatre and unites the district through the administrative offices. In this way, it emphasizes its own position within both of these larger-scale entities. As a historical structure, the town also benefits from the accentuation of subtle spatial forms and networks of routes, not to mention the creation of a new central theatre at a time when the closure of many such institutions is on the agenda. One sees that the process of urban transformation allows sensitive links to manifest themselves: among other things, the old Horten store is concealed within the new building. The conversion scheme in Neuss is a model of its kind in general terms because it cannot be so in concrete terms: despite the large number of department stores elsewhere which, after an initial conversion to new uses, have not yet seriously embarked on a second life, one cannot imagine the present situation being repeated. The project in Neuss lives from its specific response to local needs and a fortunate convergence of constructional and functional urban factors. This, in turn, calls for further town planning measures.

Während sich der Raum im Theaterfoyer frei entfaltet, betonen die Stahlbetonträger und neu geschaffenen Brücken im Kreishaus die Längsausrichtung des dortigen ›Atriums‹. Weite Glasflächen führen derweil das Licht tief in den einst ganz nach innen gewendeten Baukörper; Büros und Säle profitieren von der ungewöhnlichen lichten Höhe von bis zu 3,50 Metern.

While the theatre foyer unfolds in a spatially free form, the reinforced concrete beams and newly inserted bridges in the district administration tract accentuate the linearity of the atrium. Broad areas of glazing allow daylight to penetrate deep into what was formerly a wholly introverted building. The offices and hall spaces benefit from the unusually great room height of up to 3.50 m.

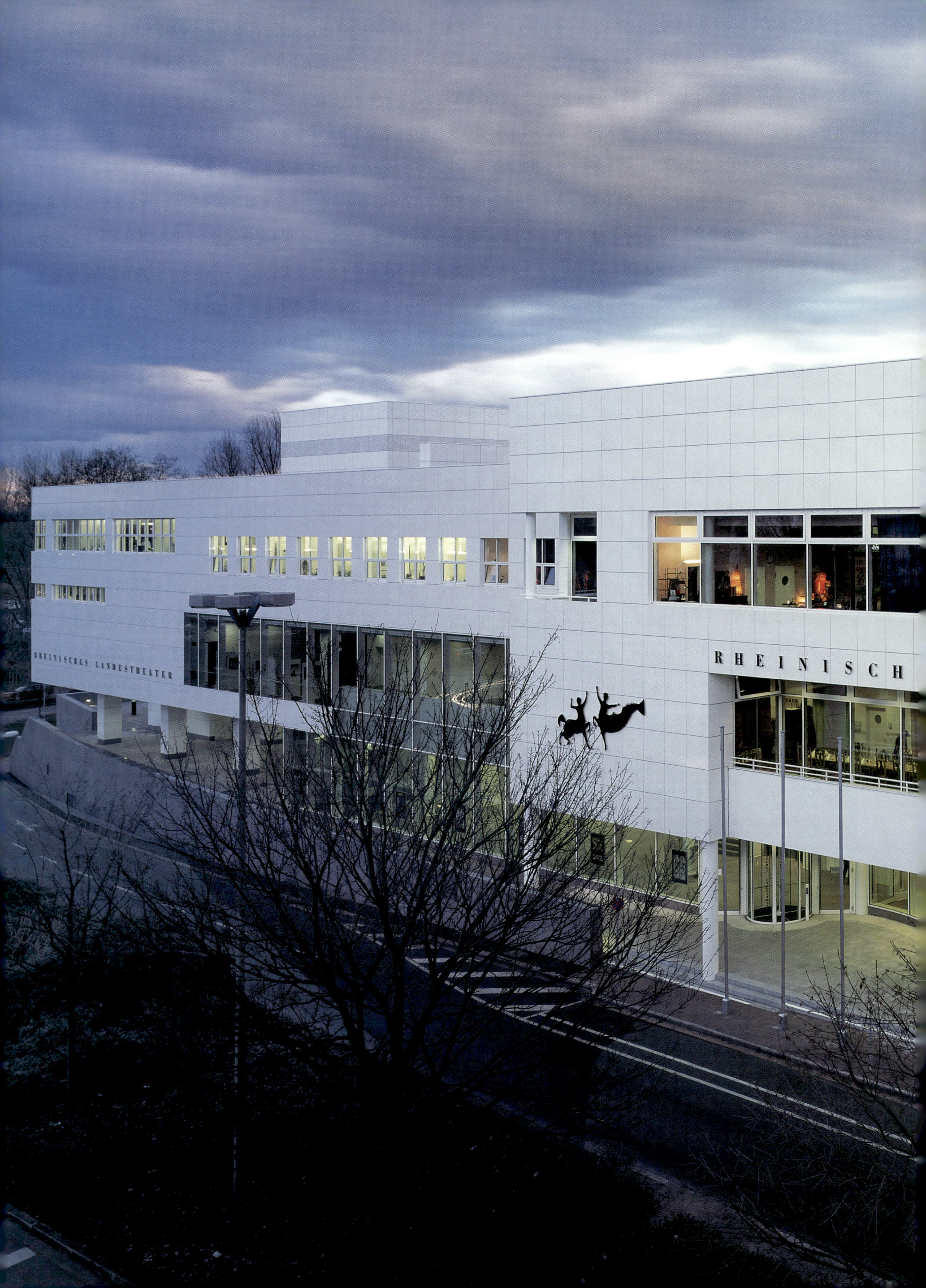
RHEINISCHES LANDESTHEATER
RHEINISCH

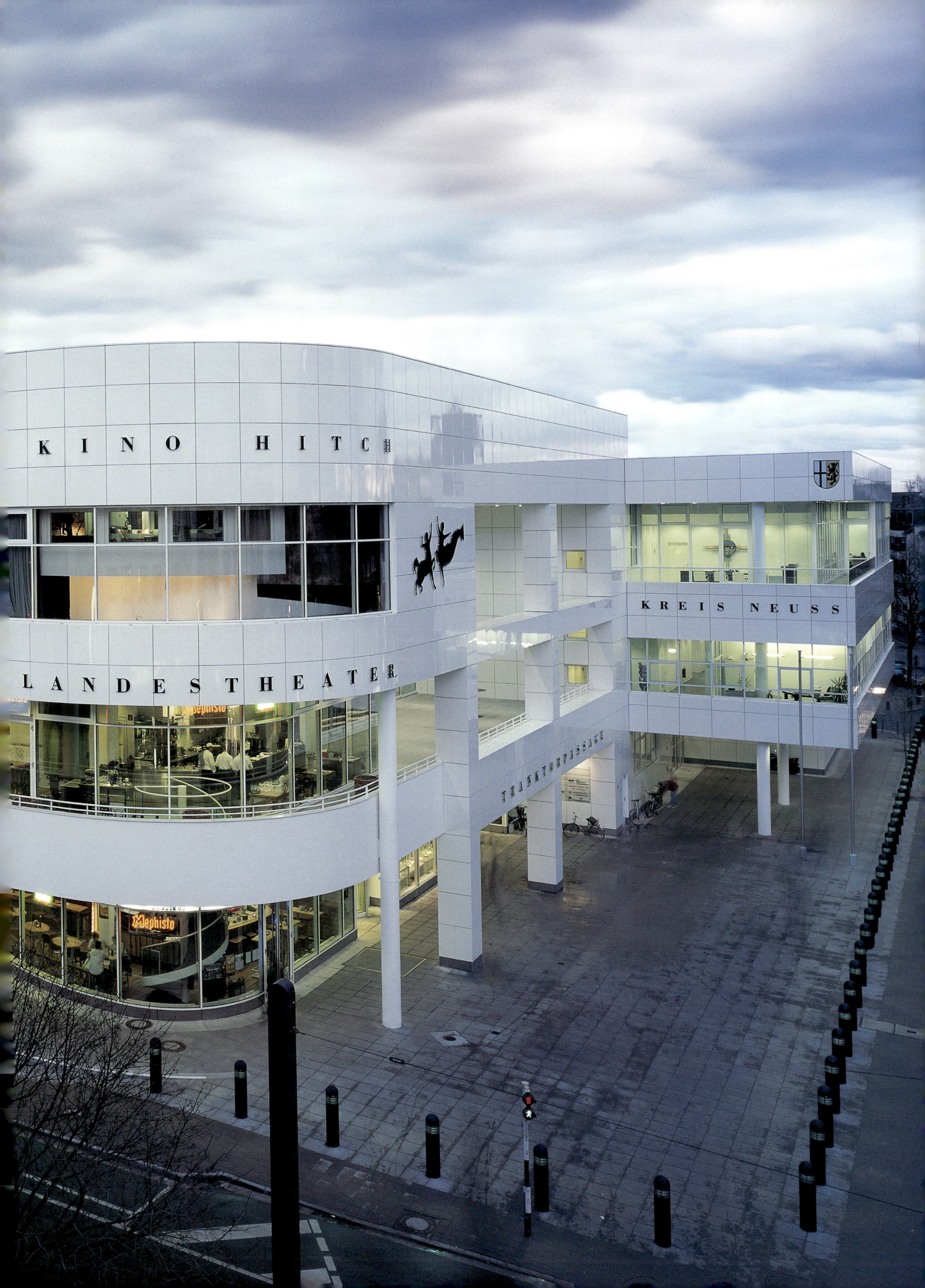
KINO HITCH
LANDESTHEATER
KREIS NEUSS
Mephisto

Blick vom Gelände des obsolet gewordenen Busbahnhofs: Der geöffnete Baukörper mit dahinter liegendem Foyer antizipiert bereits Planungen, die ein attraktives Gegenüber schaffen und die Vehemenz der Verkehrsschneise mildern könnten. Der Entwurf der Architekten sieht eine Fußgängerbrücke in diese Richtung vor.

View from the site of the abandoned bus station: the open volume of the building, with a glimpse of the foyer behind the facade, anticipates planning that could create an attractive vis-à-vis and reduce the impact of the traffic artery. The architects' design also foresees a pedestrian bridge in this direction.

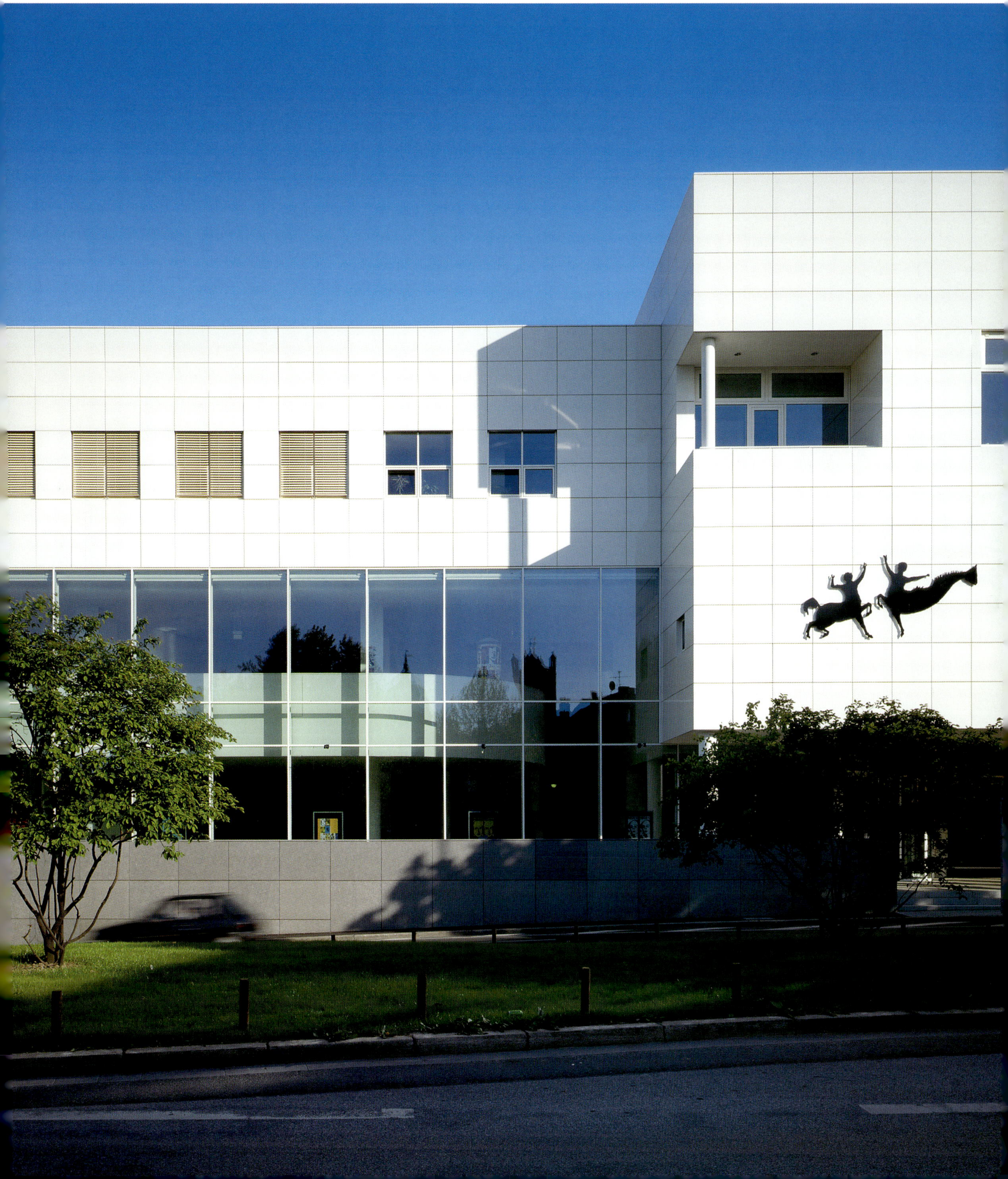

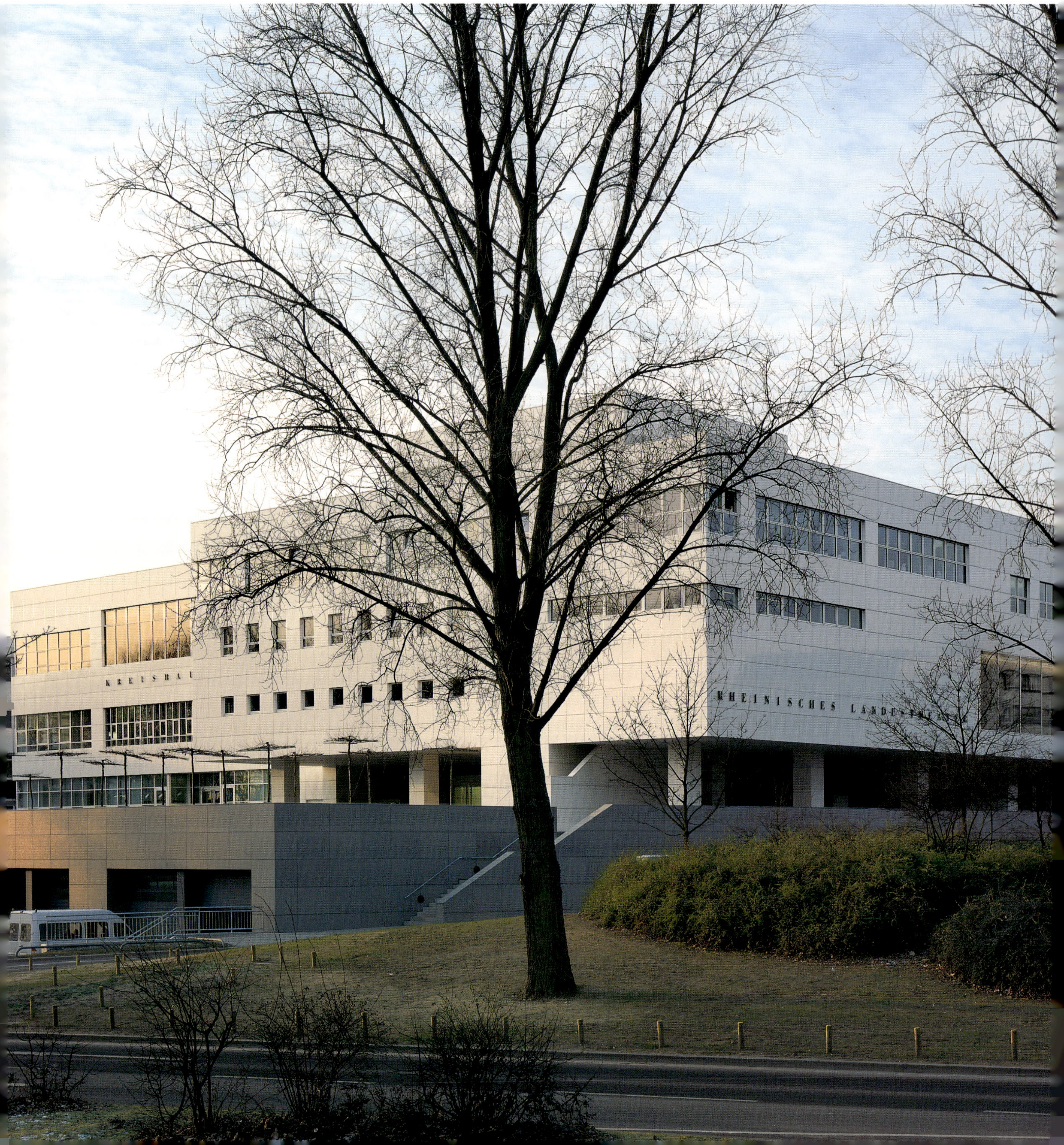
RHEINISCHES

Auch die Treppe von der Terrasse hinab zum Europadamm zeugt von den Bemühungen, städtebauliche Anschlüsse zu ermöglichen. Der neue ›Organismus‹ bedeutet eine Hypothek, die erst durch die Anbindung derzeitiger Problemzonen wie des teilverwaisten Hafens im Norden eingelöst würde.

The stairs leading down from the terrace to the Europadamm are also evidence of the efforts to create urban links. The new "organism" is a commitment; the debt will be redeemed only when problem areas like the partly derelict harbour to the north are integrated into the urban tissue.

Die harte Kante entlang des Europa-
damms folgt den Spuren der einstigen
Stadtmauer – und entspricht den
Umrissen des vorgefundenen Unter-
geschosses. Die Fläche darüber
wurde mit zurückhaltenden Mitteln
und Platanen in geordneter Aufstellung
als Freiraum für die Stadt gewonnen.

The hard edge of the development
along the Europadamm follows the
lines of the former town walls and
the retained basement of the former
building. With modest means and
a symmetrical arrangement of plane
trees, it was possible to reclaim the
area above the basement as public
urban space.

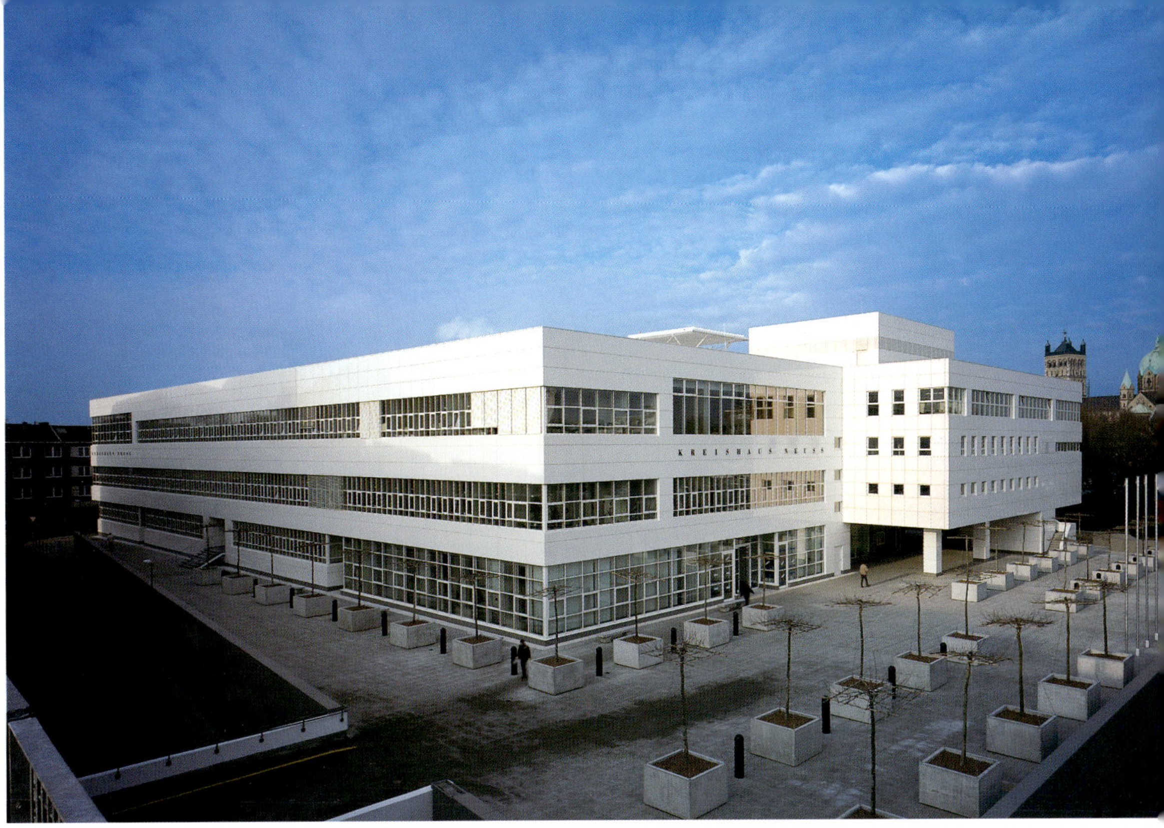

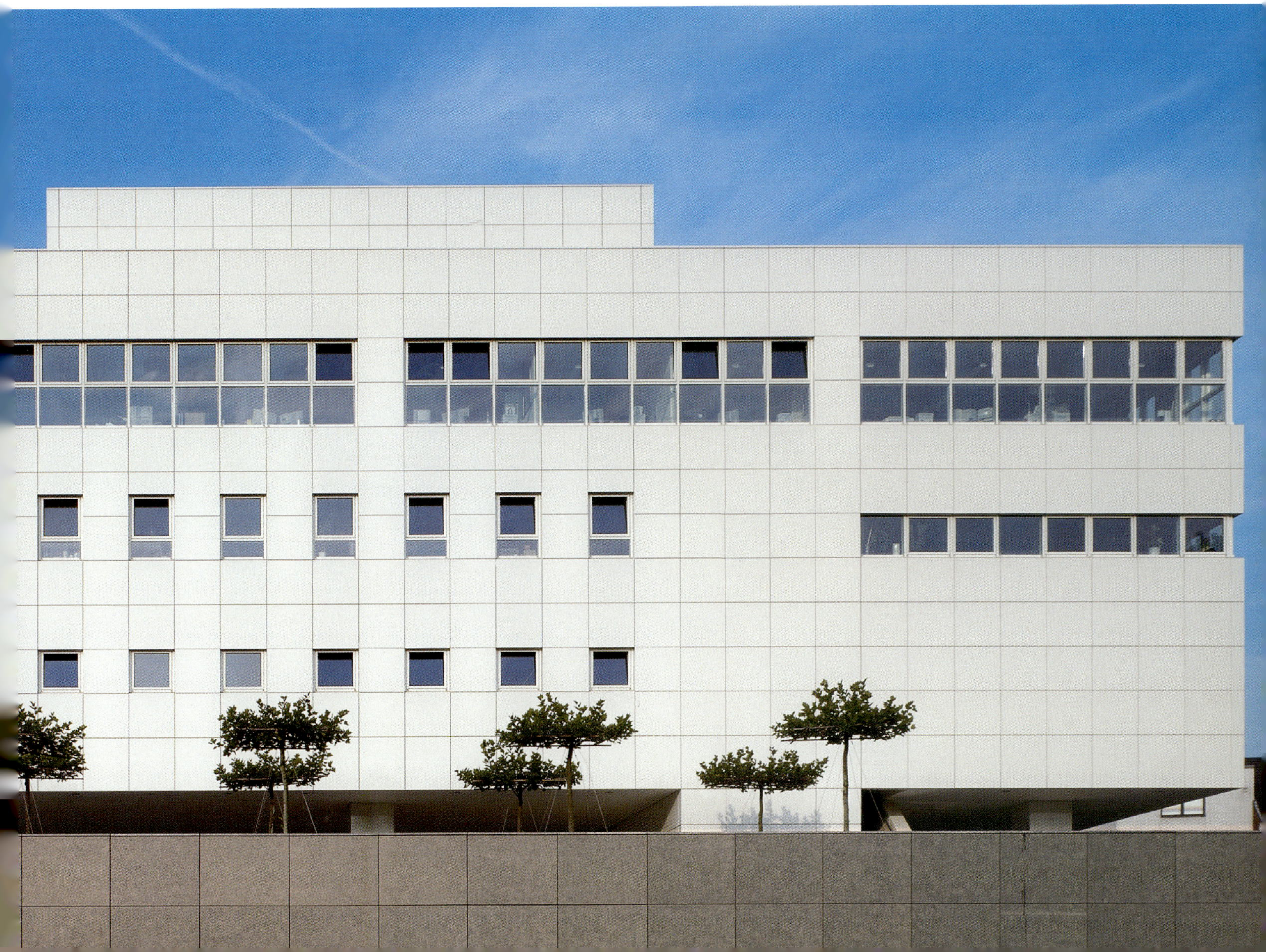

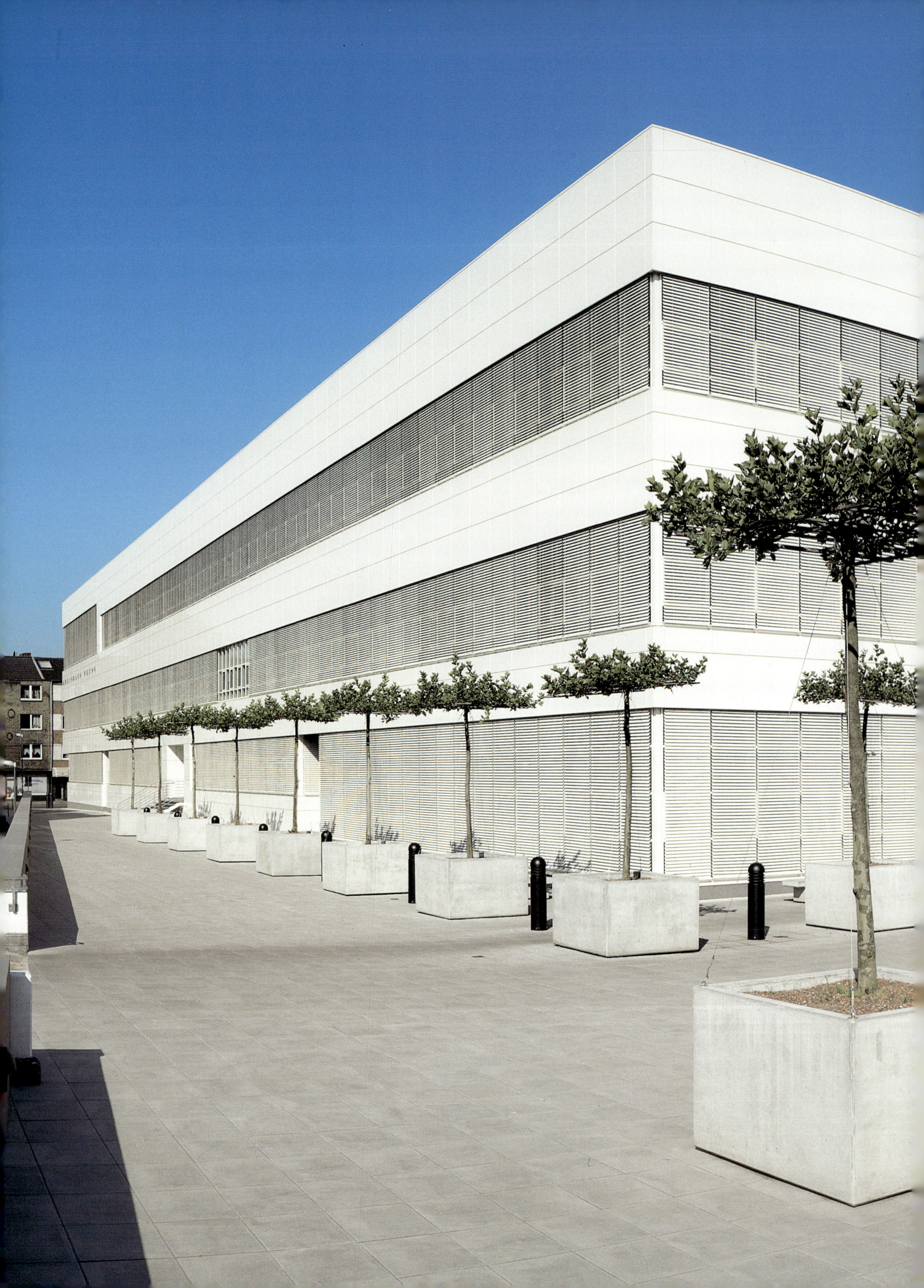

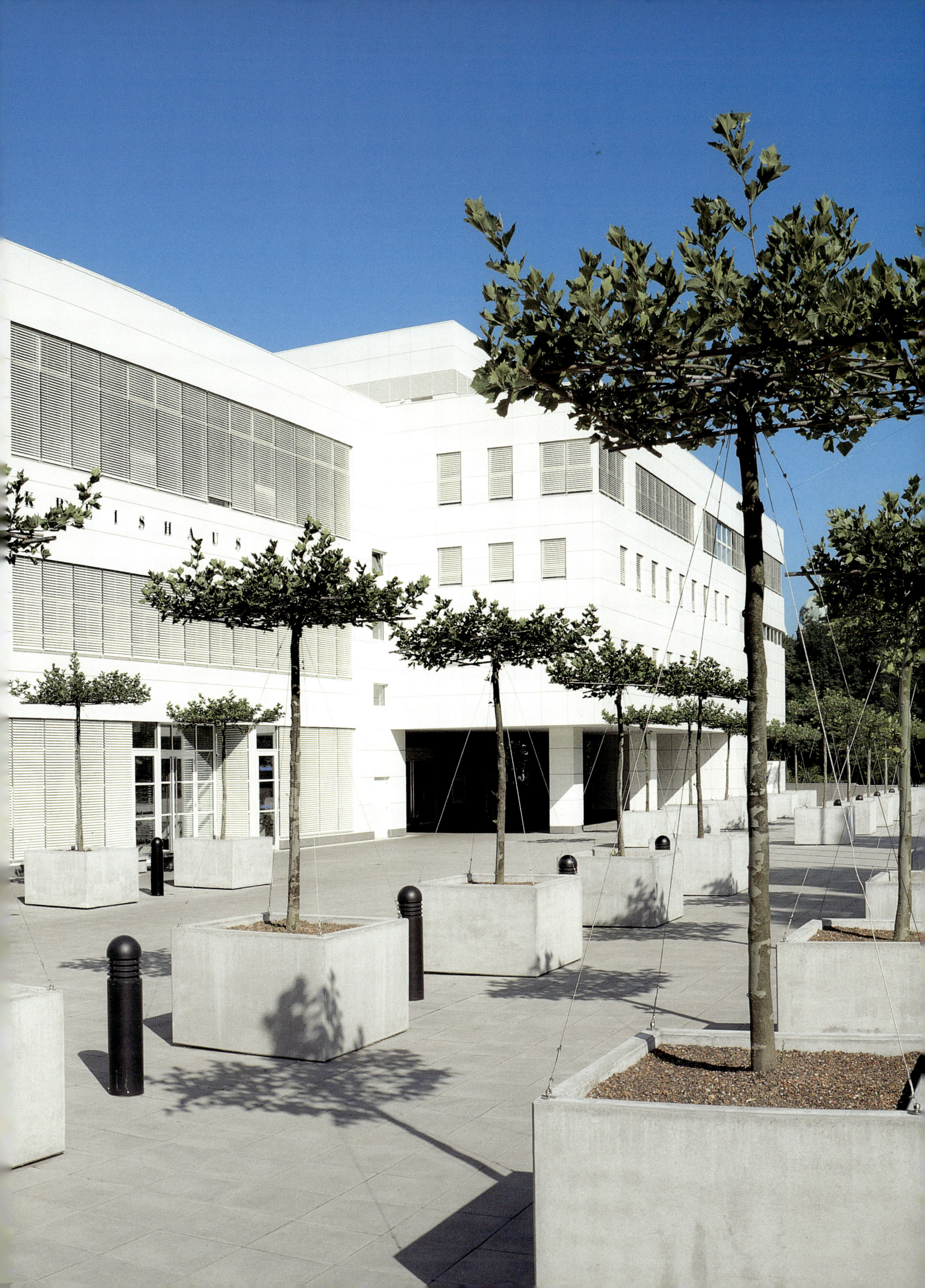

Stadtabgewandt entwickelt die Fassade eine klare, gradlinige Dynamik. Ungebrochene ›schnelle‹ Fensterbänder greifen um die Gebäudeecke herum und künden vom statischen System mit zurückversetzten Stützen. Der außenliegende Sonnenschutz und das Raster der einbrennlackierten Leichtmetallhaut fördern die Abstraktion.

The side of the development facing away from the town centre has its own clear, linear dynamics. Continuous strip windows sweep along the face of the building and round the corners, signifying a structural system with columns set back from the facade. The external sunblinds and the grid of stove-enamelled lightweight metal panels accentuate the abstract quality of the overall form.

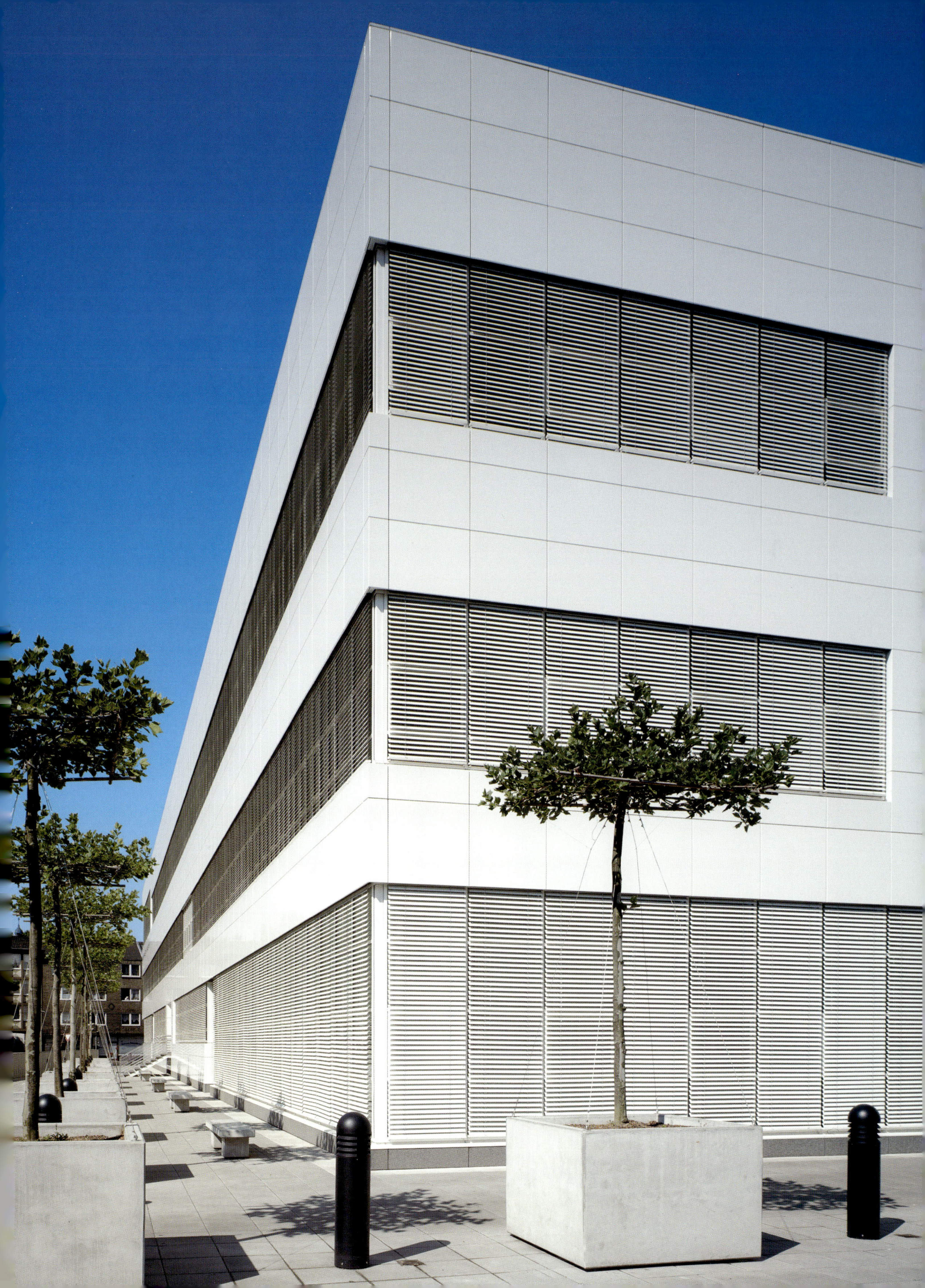

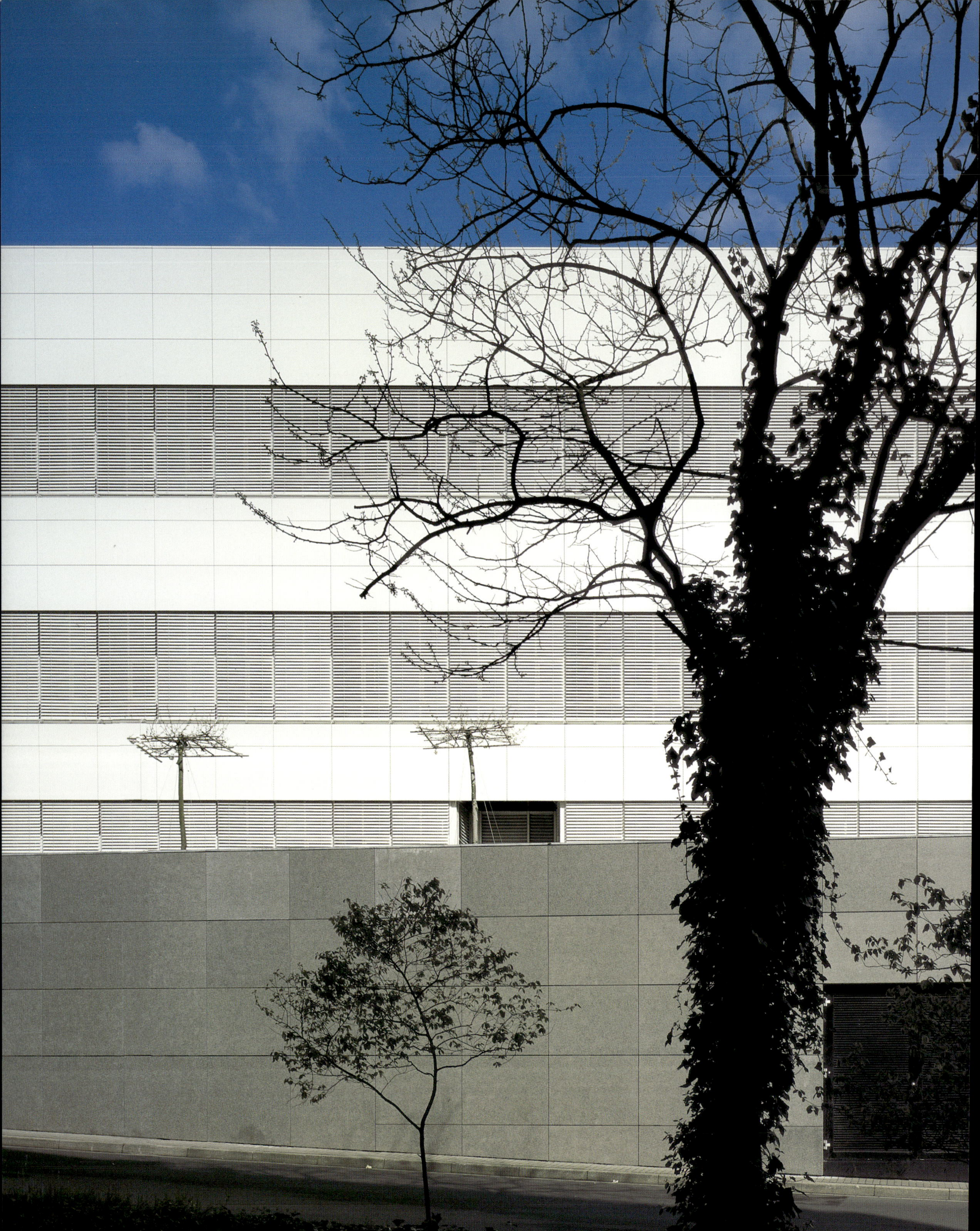

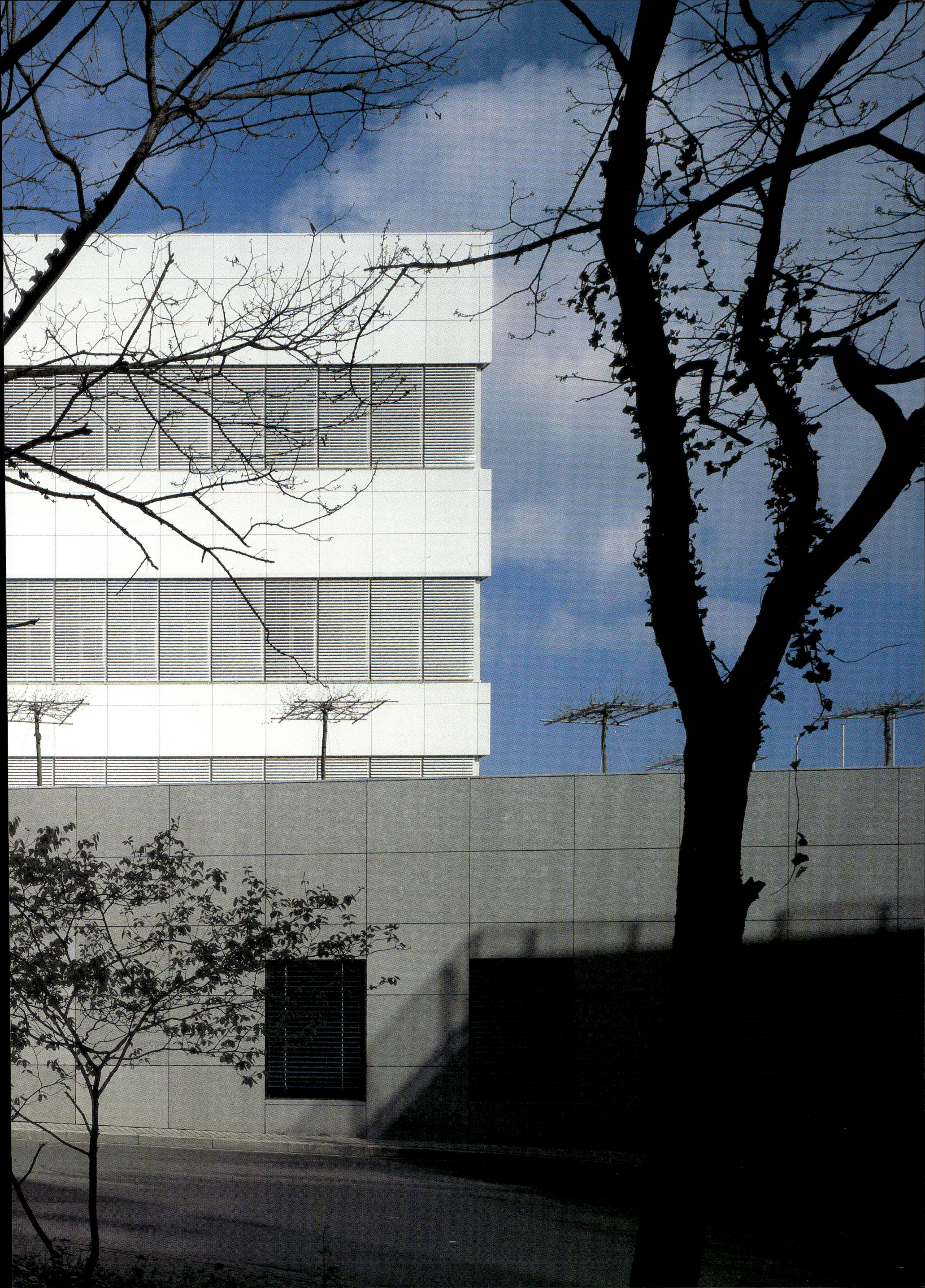

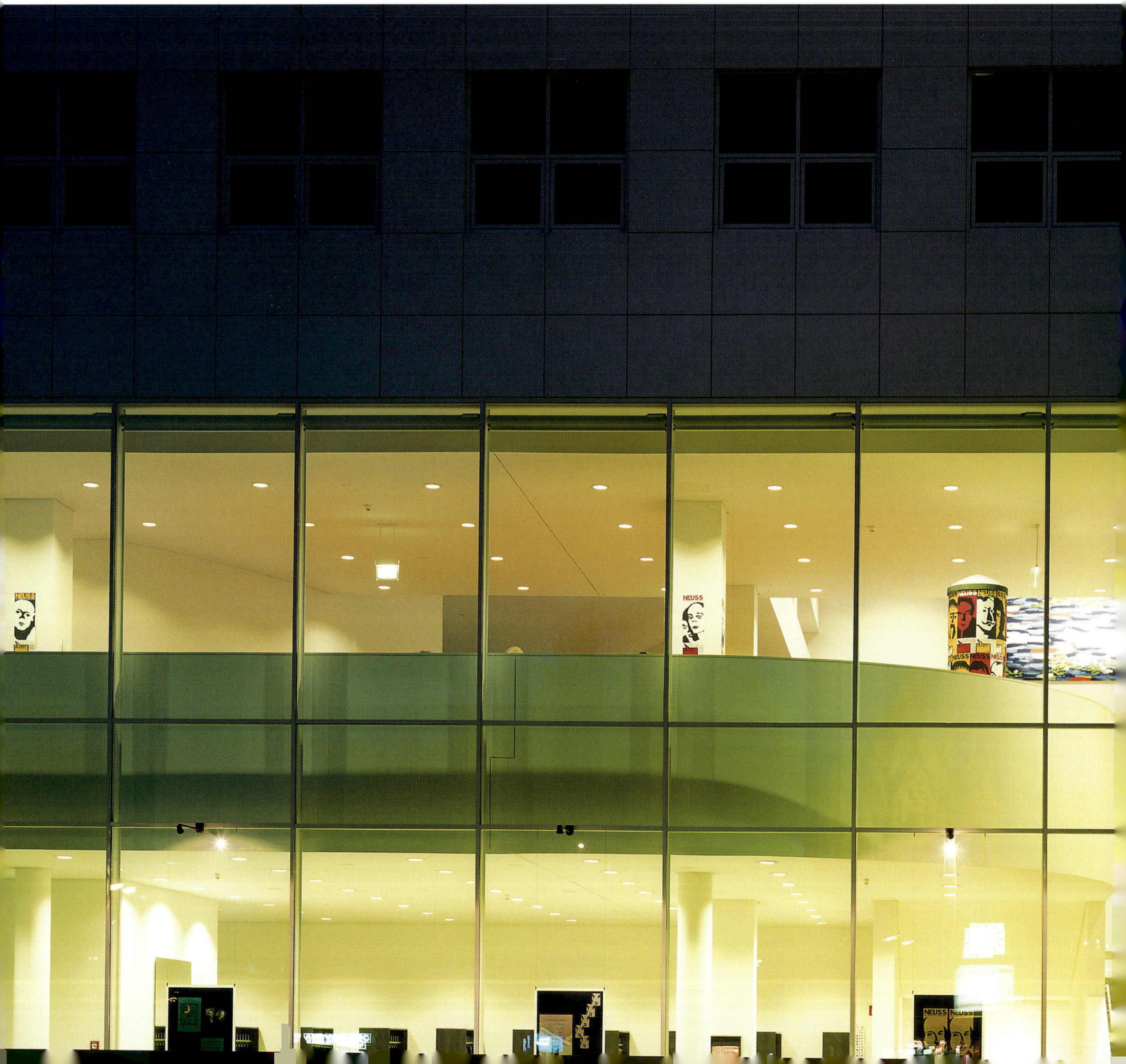
NEUSS
NEUSS
NEUSS
NEUSS NEUSS

Die Integration der verschiedenen Funktionen war zunächst durchaus umstritten und erhöhte noch den Anspruch insbesondere des Theaters an eine repräsentative Gestalt. Bauliche und inszenatorische Elemente verbinden sich: die unerwartete Plastizität der Fassade, Transparenz und die Verlockungen nächtlicher Beleuchtung, die das Innere des Foyers in die Stadt hinein zu rücken scheinen.

The integration of the various functions was initially a contentious issue and actually strengthened the claims, especially on the part of the theatre, to a prestigious formal appearance. Constructional and dramatically staged elements unite to lend the facade a surprising three-dimensionality. Transparency and the attractions of nocturnal lighting seem to project the interior of the foyer out into the urban surroundings.

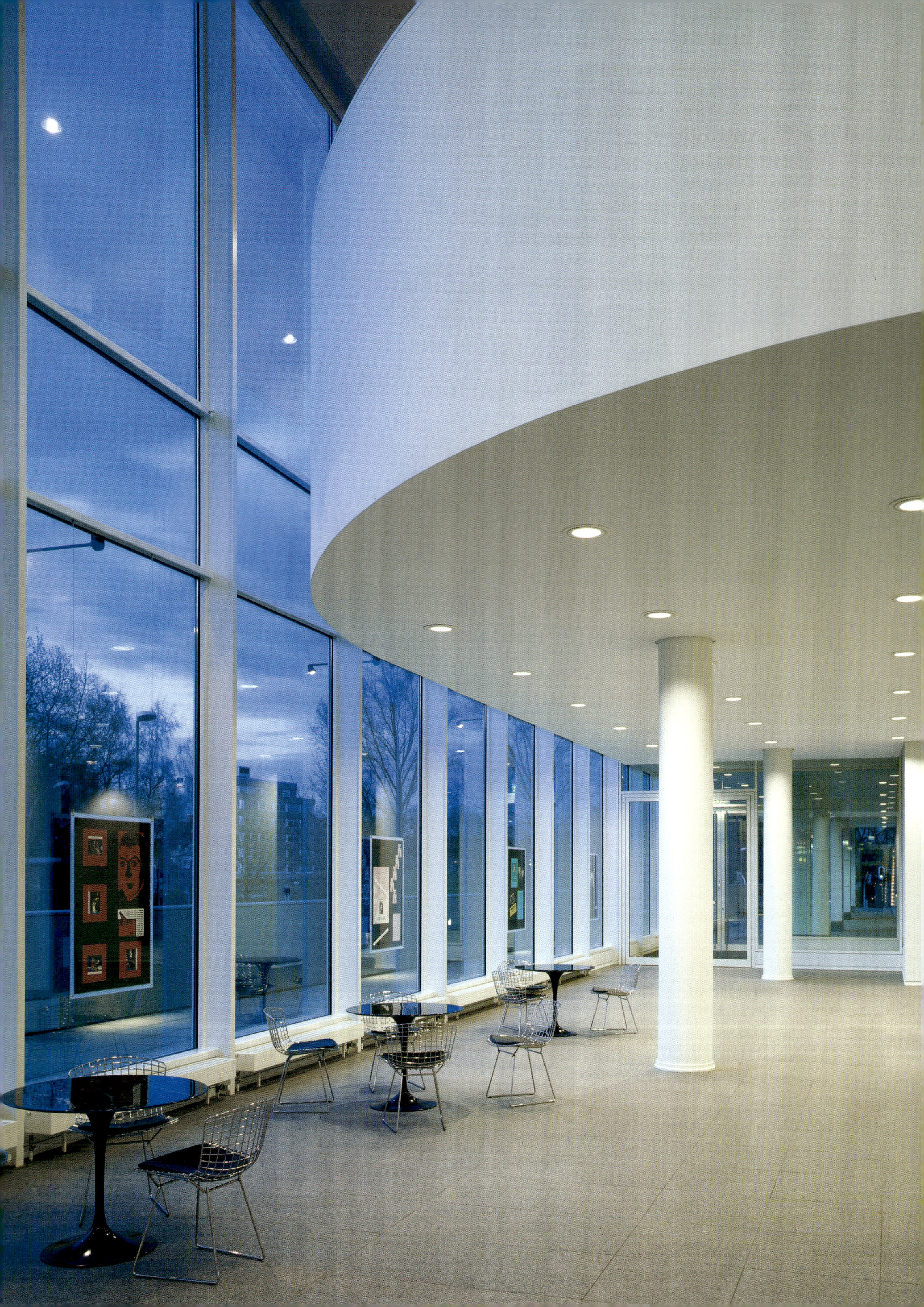

Die Architekten taten gut daran, im Inneren Zurückhaltung walten zu lassen. Statt aufwändiger Materialien bestimmen klare architektonische Formen den Raumeindruck im Schauspielhaus. Vom Parterre mit Garderobenfoyer und Abendkasse über die Treppe hinauf zum eigentlichen Foyer entsteht ein räumliches Kontinuum.

The architects did well to exercise restraint in the interior design. In the theatre, the spatial mood is determined by clear architectural forms, not opulent materials. A spatial continuum is created that extends from the ground floor with the cloakroom vestibule and box office, via the staircase, to the first floor.

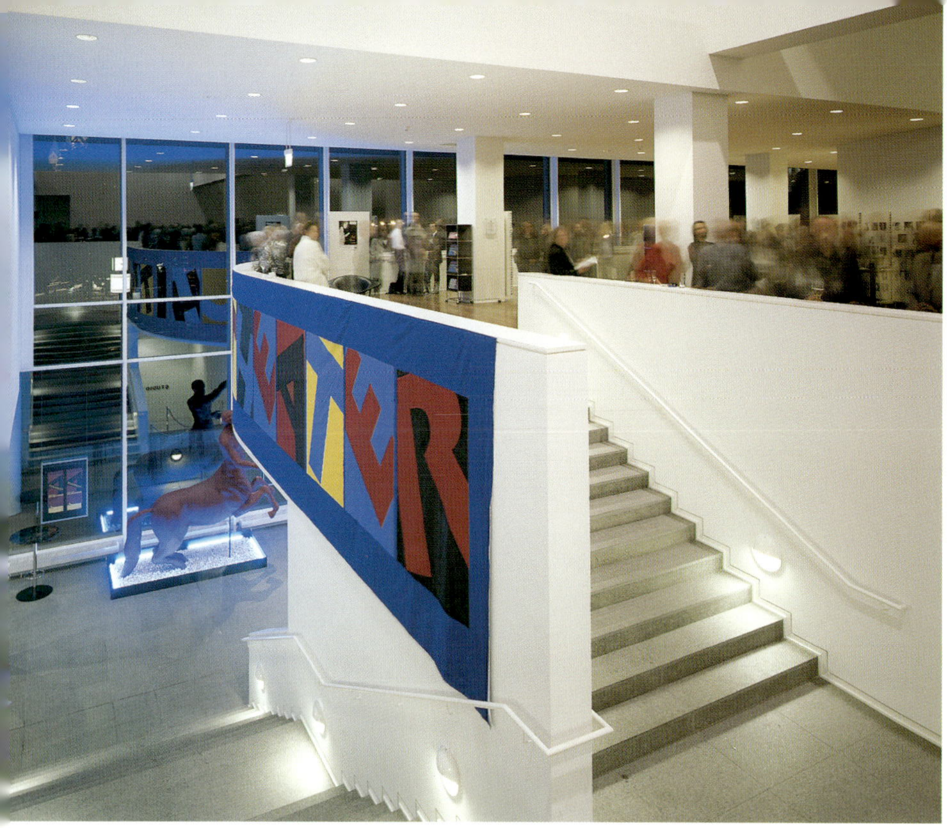

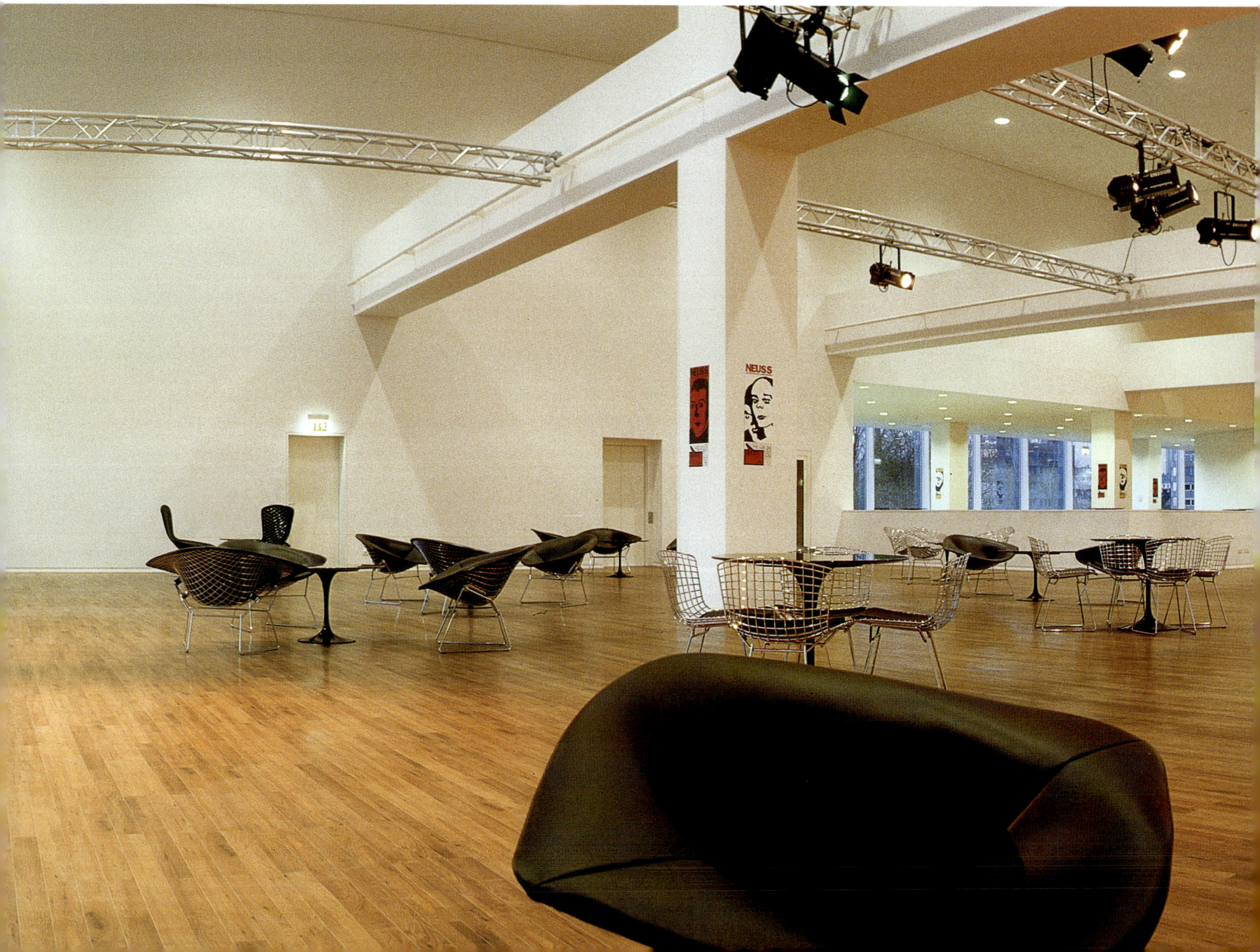
NEUSS

Das Foyer ist mit Teak ausgelegt, die Bar unter der Schräge des Zuschauerraums eingestellt. Der kaum dekorierte Raum wird vom angrenzenden Restaurant gastronomisch betreut und kann – Lichttechnik und der Vorhang deuten es an – für Veranstaltungen genutzt werden.

The foyer is finished with teak flooring. The bar is inserted beneath the raking floor of the theatre auditorium. The foyer space reveals an almost total lack of ornamentation. It is served from the adjoining restaurant and can also be used for special events, as the lighting design and the curtain suggest.

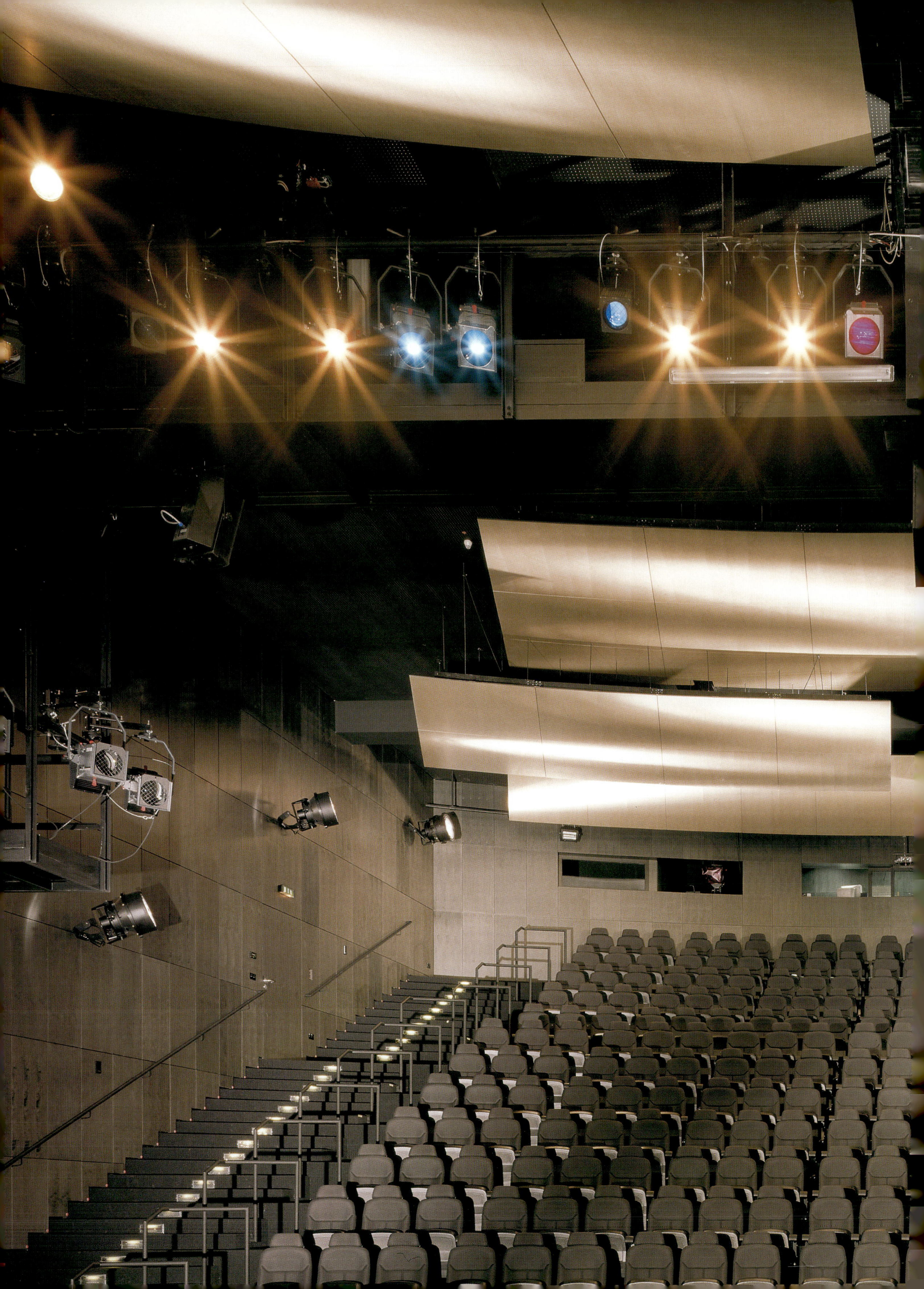

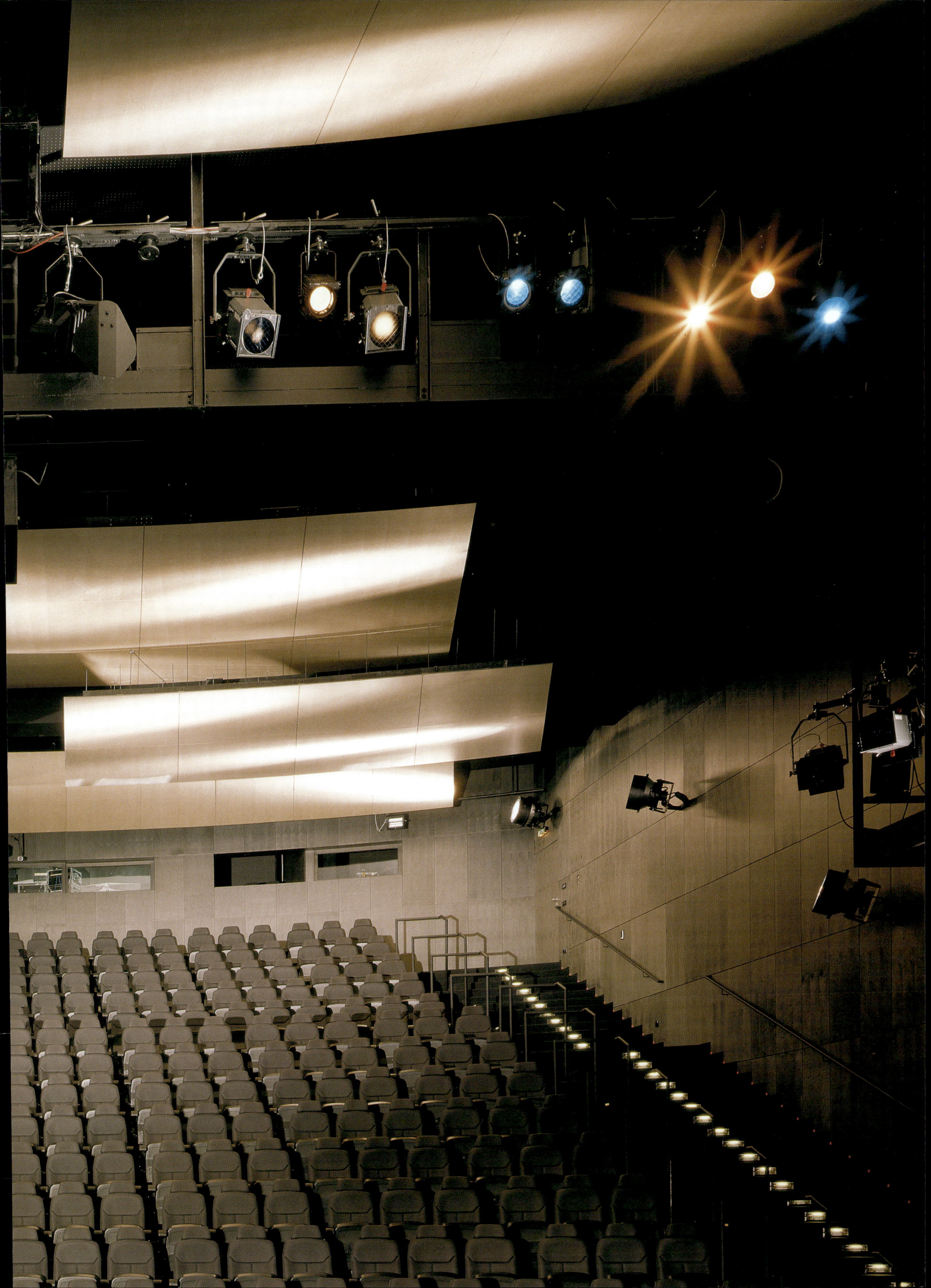

Im Herzen des Hauses:
450 Zuschauer finden auf den ansteigenden Rängen des Theatersaals Platz; dunkel eingefärbte Birkenholzvertäfelungen und unprätentiös geschnittene, helle Holzsegel unter der Decke lenken die Konzentration auf die 16 Meter breite Bühne und das dramatische Geschehen.

At the heart of the complex is the theatre, with a rising tier of seats for an audience of 450 people. Dark-stained birch panelling and simply shaped, pale timber sails suspended from the ceiling help to focus attention on the 16-metre-wide stage and the dramatic events that take place there.

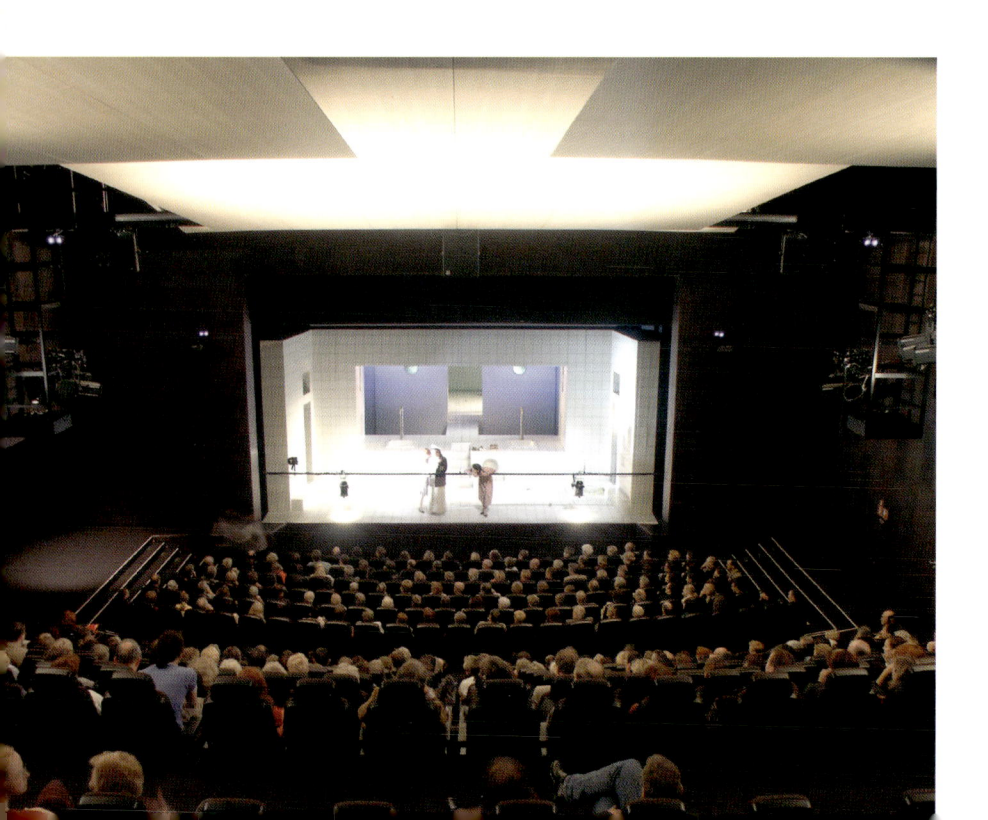

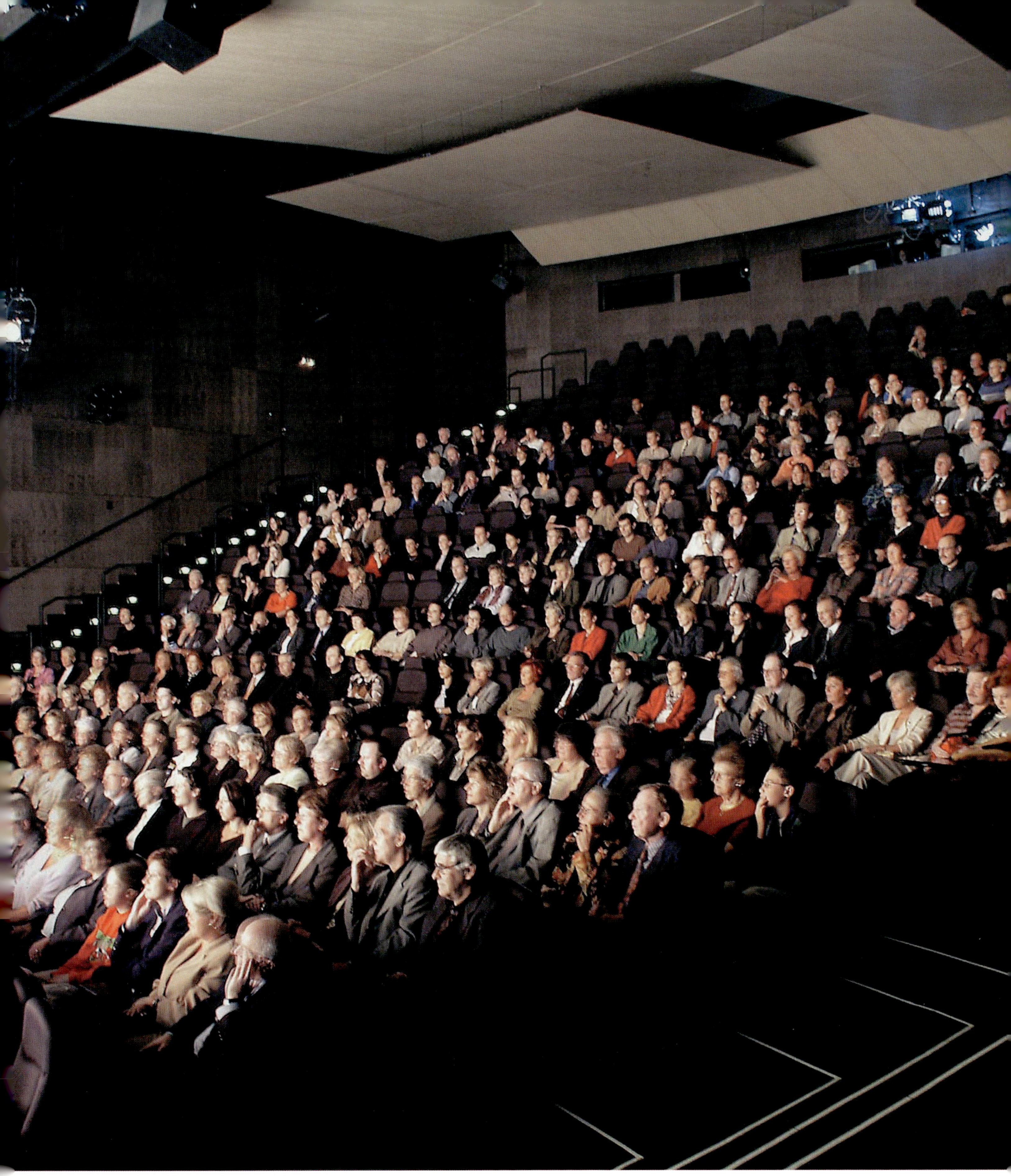

Der kleine Saal des nachträglich in das Raumprogramm aufgenommenen ›Hitch‹-Programmkinos im zweiten Obergeschoss fasst 83 Zuschauer. Mit raumhohen Fenstern, die erst zur Vorführung geschlossen werden, stellt er ein Unikum in Deutschland dar. Vom Zugang zum Saal geht der Blick hinaus durch die geschwungene Glasfassade auf die nächtliche Stadt.

The small "Hitch" arts cinema on the second floor was added to the spatial programme at a later date. It contains seating for 83 cinema-goers. With full-height windows that are blacked out only shortly before the screening of the film, it is quite unique in Germany. From the cinema entrance, the view extends out through the curved glass facade to the town by night.

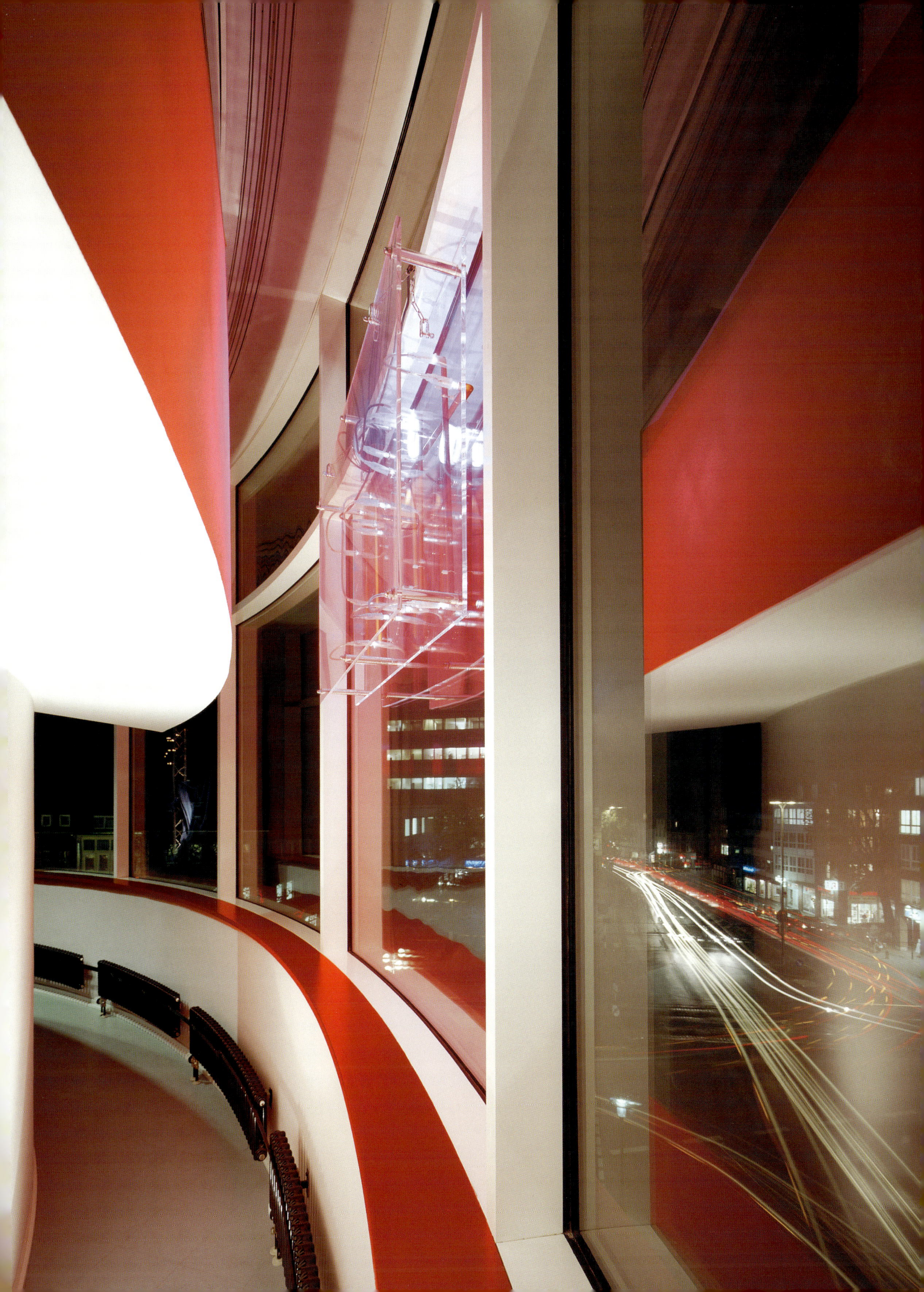

Gleiche Sprache, und doch ein anderer Duktus: Das Antlitz des Kreishauses wirkt flächiger als nebenan beim Theater, und auch das Innere weicht weniger vom Regelmaß strenger Orthogonalität ab. Die Brücken, die die hohe Halle queren, sind mit mattiertem Sicherheitsglas ausgelegt, die gläsernen Brüstungen scheinen auf den Handlauf aus weißem Aluminium reduziert.

The same language, yet a different style: the face of the district administration tract has a more planar appearance than that of the adjoining theatre. The interior, too, deviates less from the strict orthogonal structure. The floors of the elevated bridges across the hall are finished with obscured safety glass. The glazed balustrades seem reduced to little more than the white aluminium handrails.

GREVENBROICH

ROMMERSKIRCHEN

KAARST

SERVICE CENTER

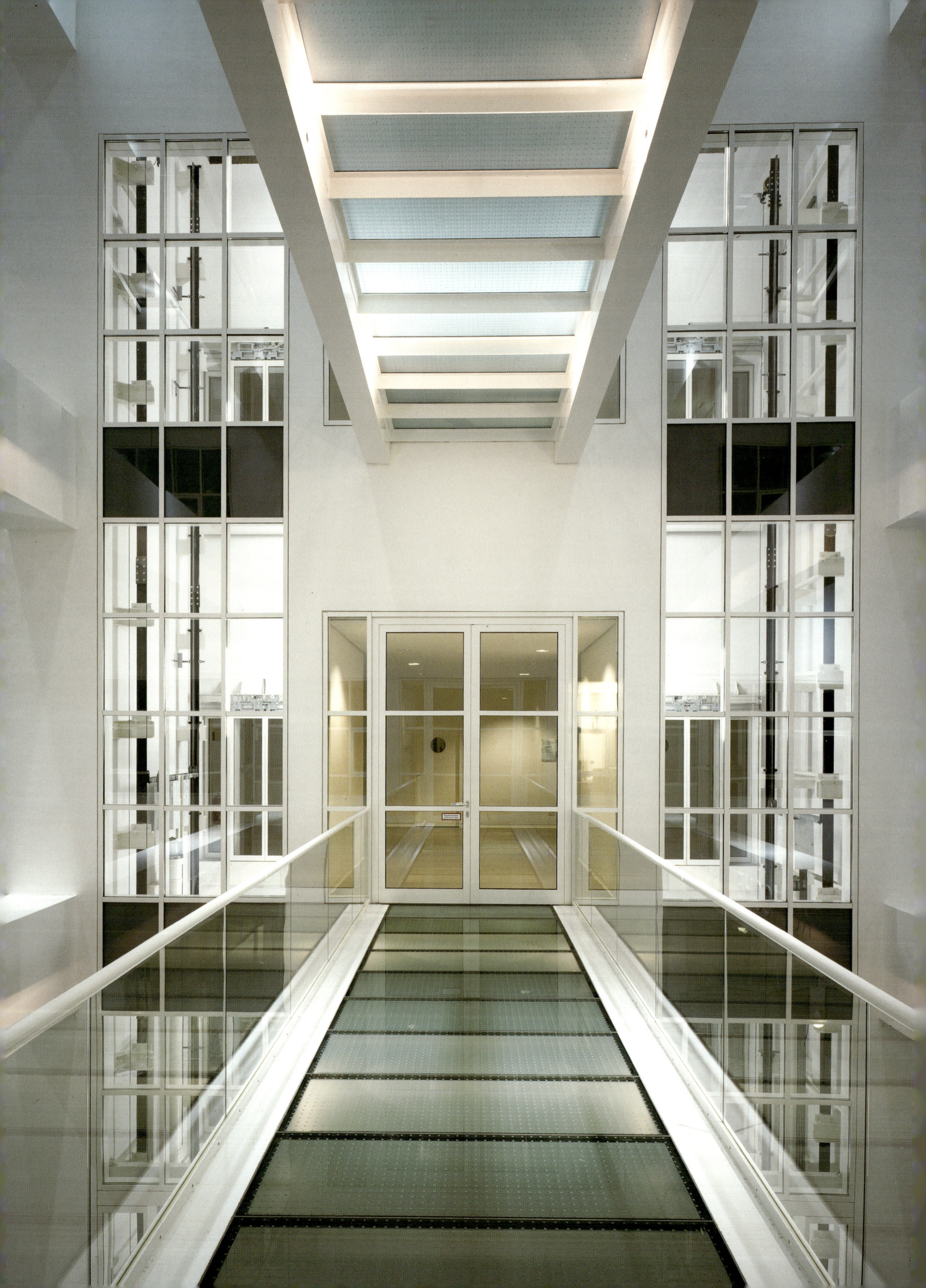

In weißen Lettern stehen die Namen der acht Städte und Gemeinden im Kreis auf den freigelegten Trägern des Stahlbetonskeletts. Dazwischen reicht der Blick 17 Meter hinauf zum Linienraster des Glasdachs und der Schraffur des aufgeständerten Sonnenschutzes. Die Lamellen folgen dem Stand der Sonne und machen Jalousien in den zur Halle orientierten Büros überflüssig.

The names of the eight towns and communities within the district are set in white letters on the exposed cross-beams of the reinforced concrete skeleton-frame structure. Between these elements, the view extends 17 metres upwards to the grid of the glazed roof and the strip-like pattern of the raised sunscreen installation on the outside. The louvres follow the position of the sun, so that no blinds are necessary in the offices facing on to the hall.

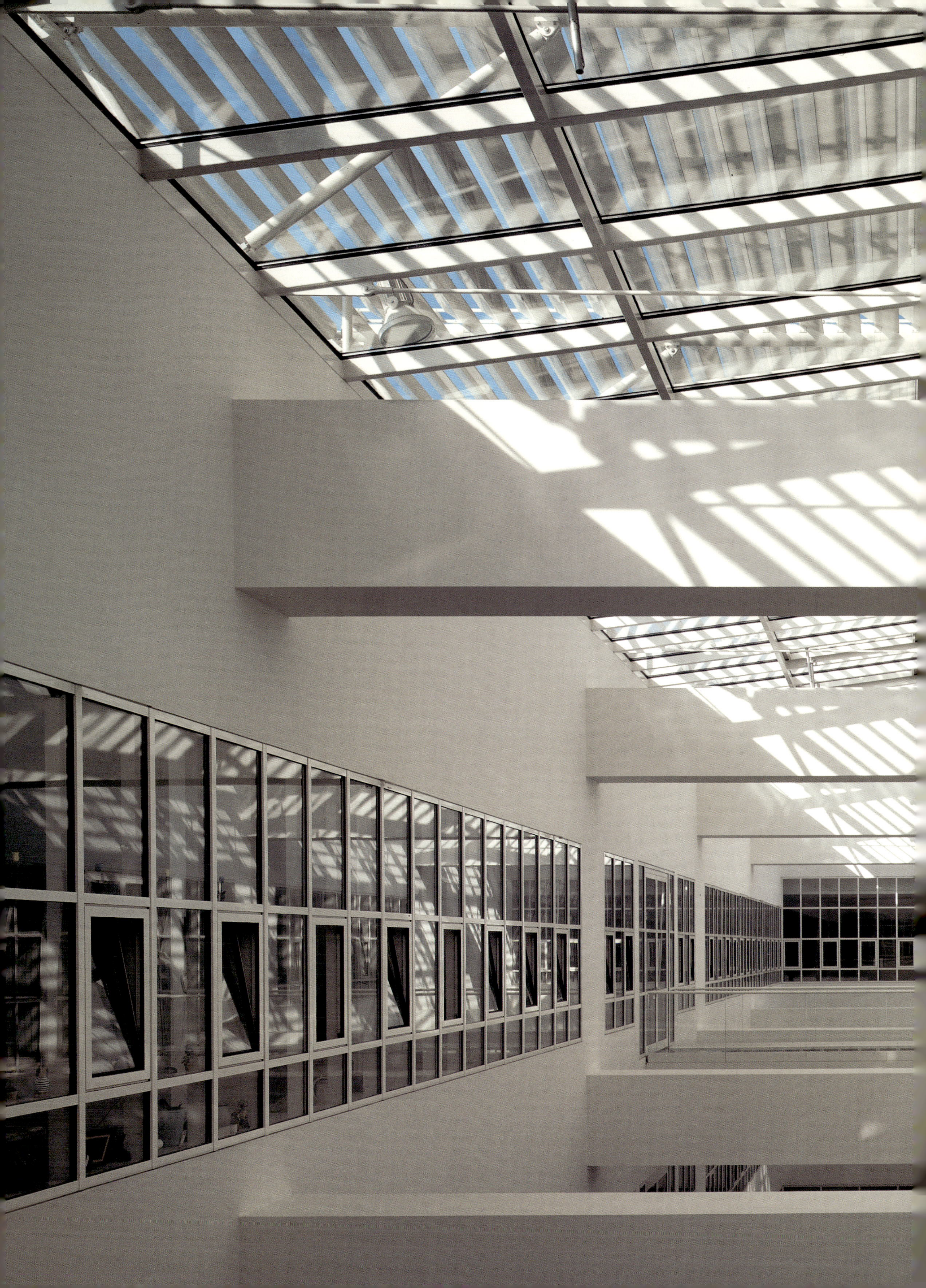

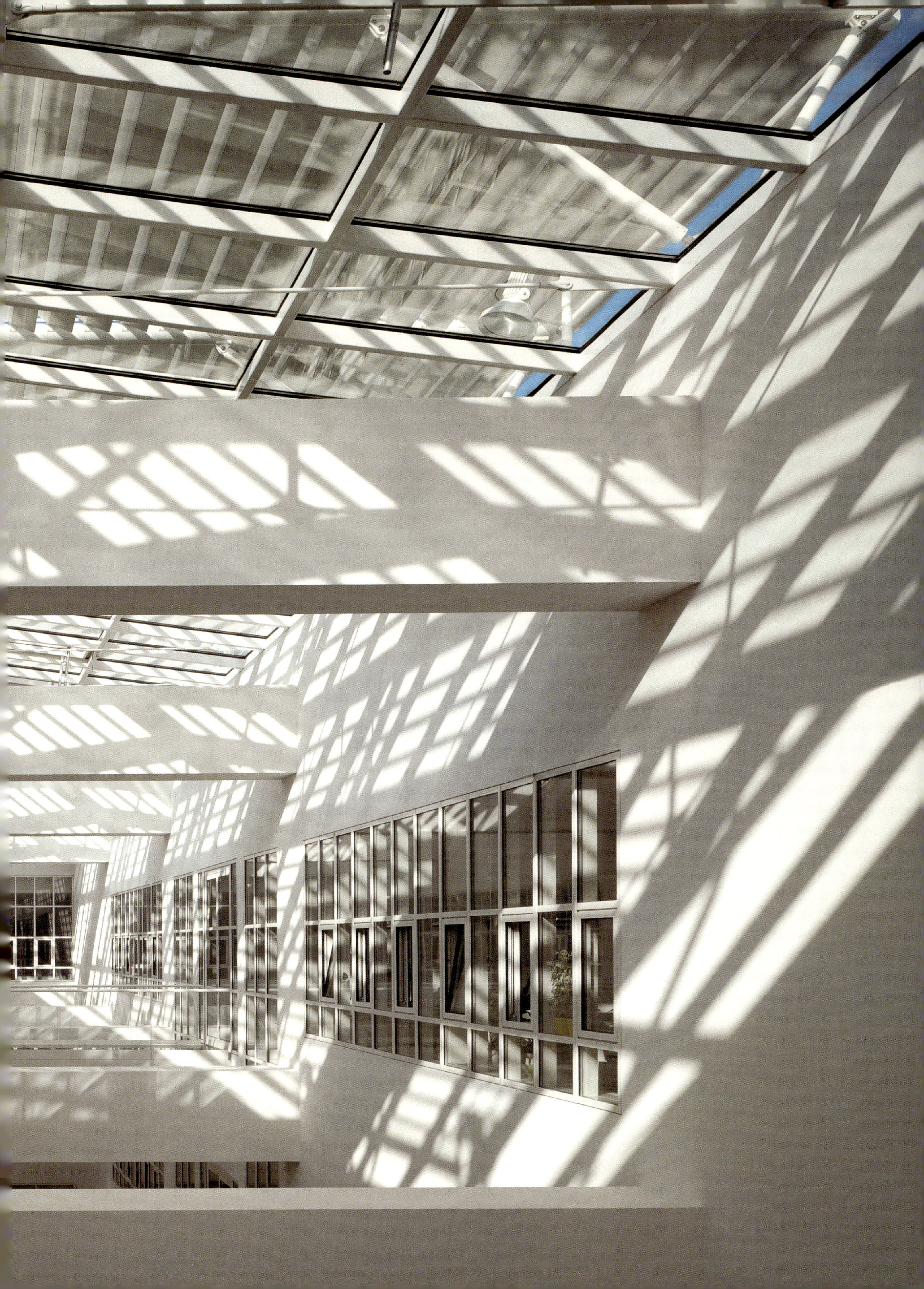

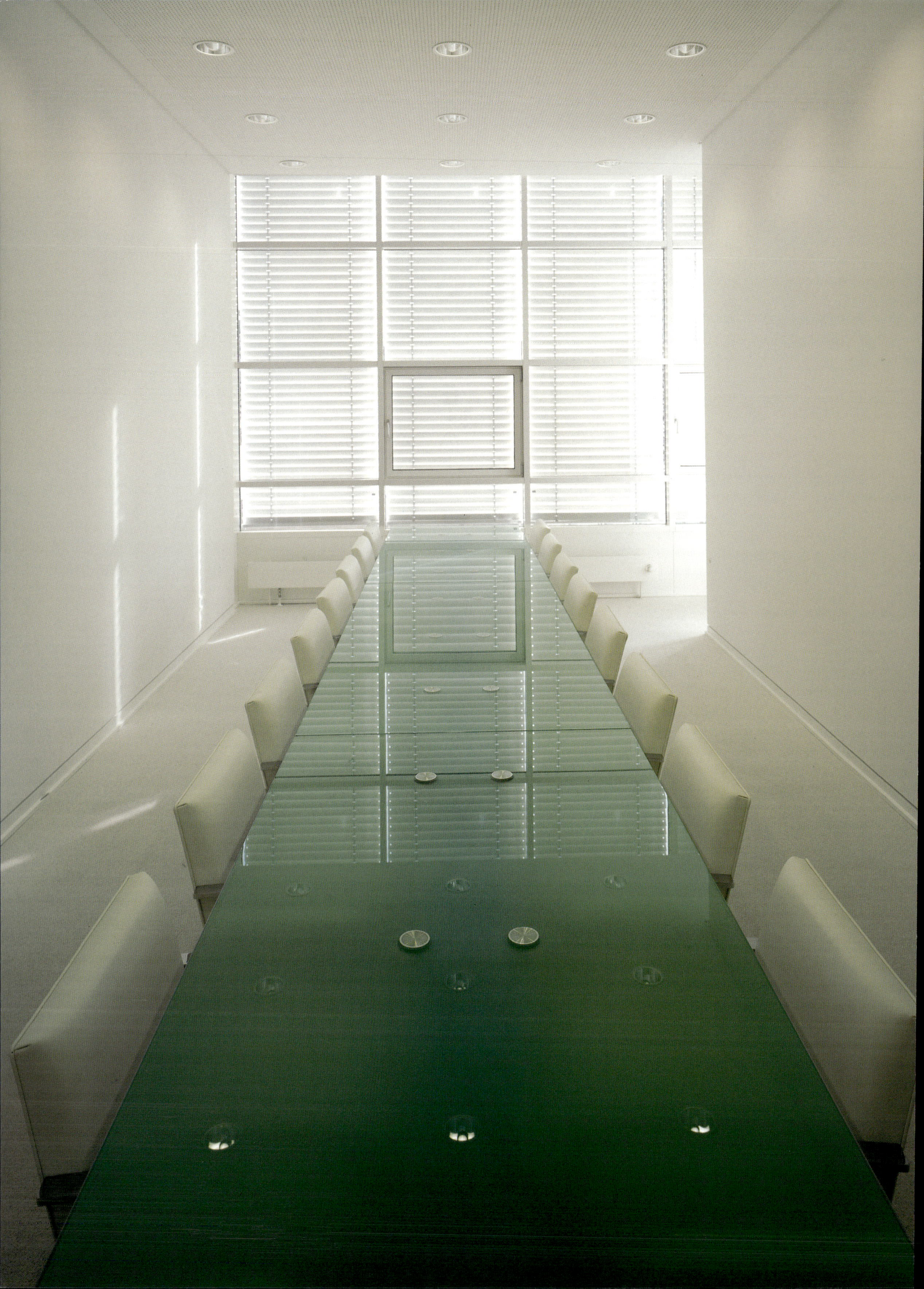

Sonnenlicht projiziert die Fassadenordnung in das schlanke, schmucklose Konferenzzimmer der Verwaltungsspitze. Den großen Sitzungsraum, ebenfalls im zweiten Obergeschoss gelegen, krönt eine vier Meter weite Lichtkuppel; Faltschiebe-Trennwände rechts und links erlauben die Erweiterung zum dreischiffigen Saal.

Sunlight projects the patterns of the facade structure into the narrow, unadorned conference room for the heads of the administration. The large conference room, also on the second floor, is crowned by a domed skylight four metres in diameter. Folding-sliding wall elements to left and right allow the space to be enlarged into a three-bay hall.

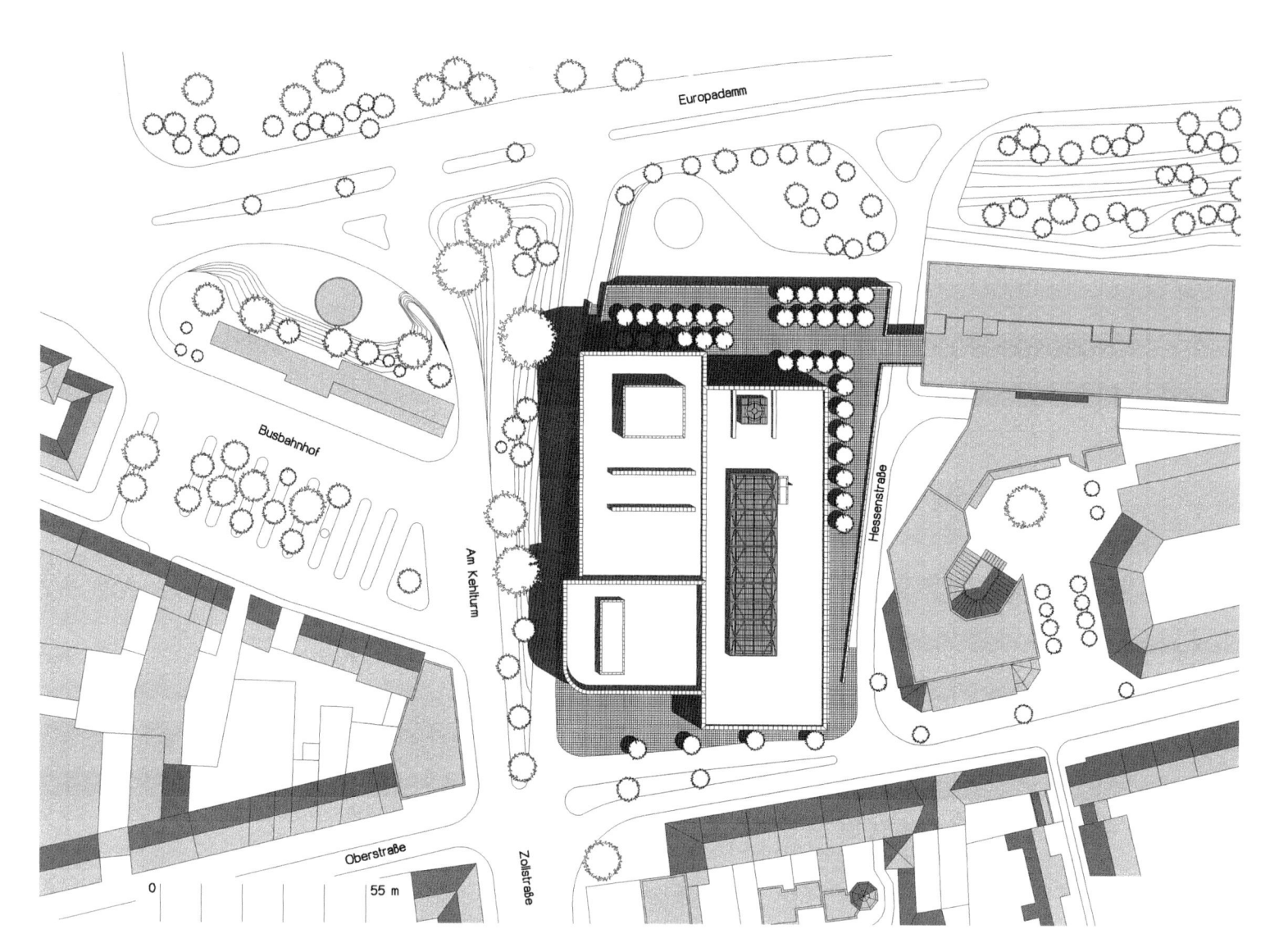

Lageplan / Site plan

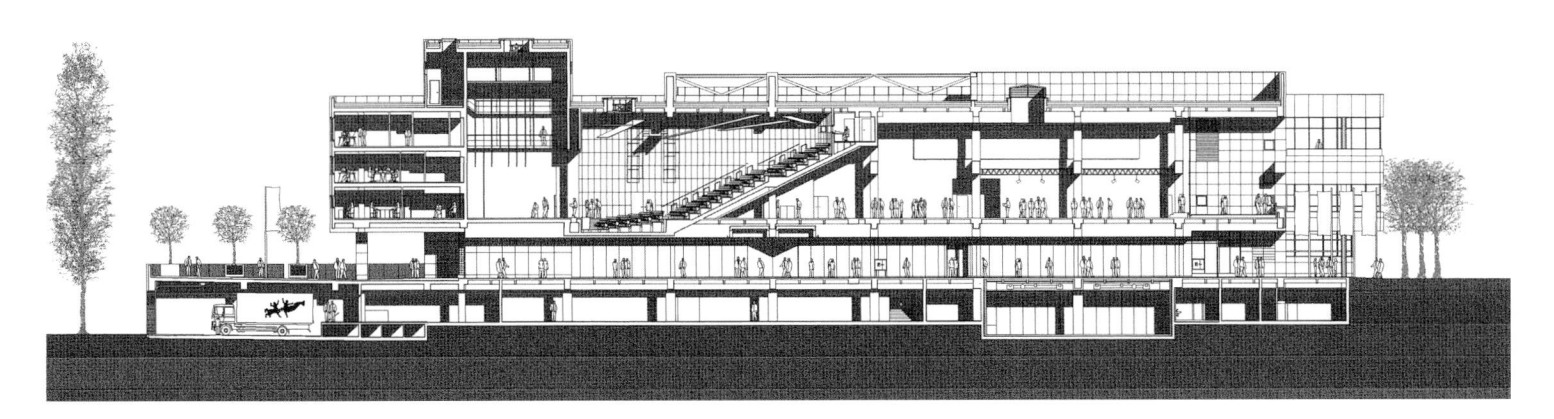

Längsschnitt Theater / Longitudinal section through theatre

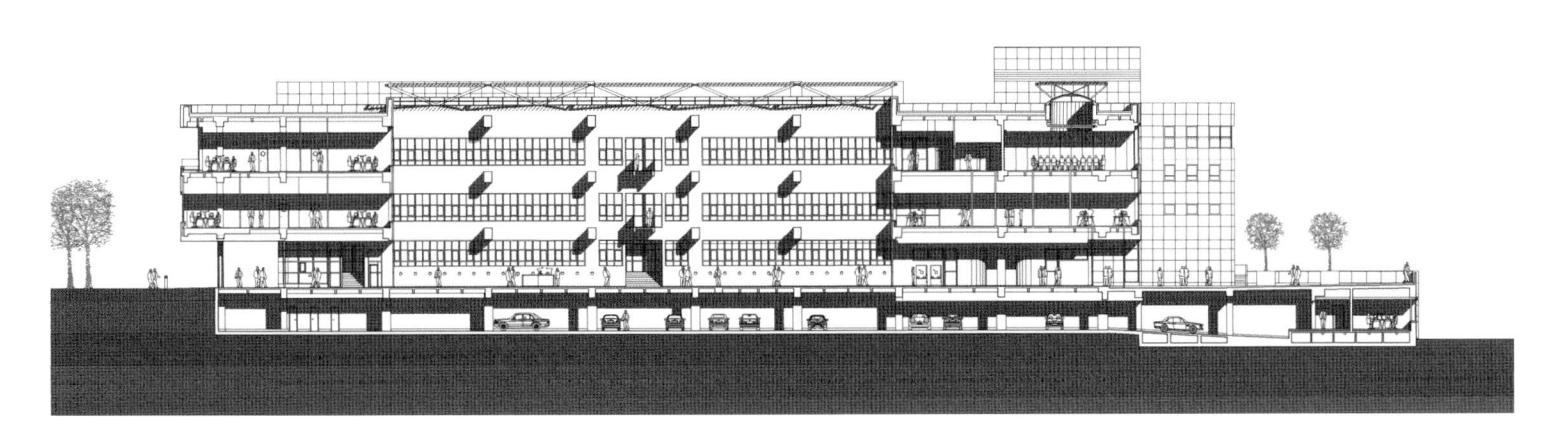

Längsschnitt Kreisverwaltung / Longitudinal section through district administration

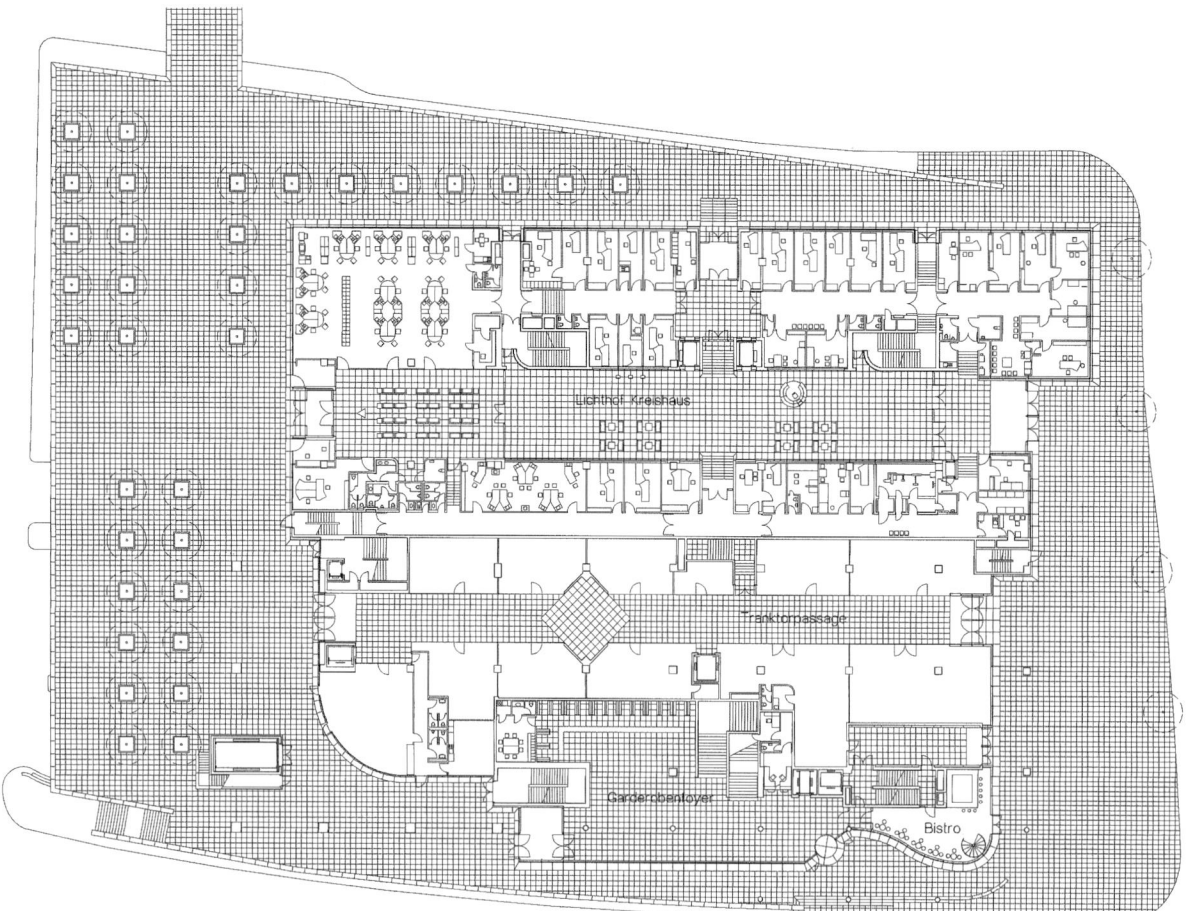

Grundriss Erdgeschoss / Ground floor plan

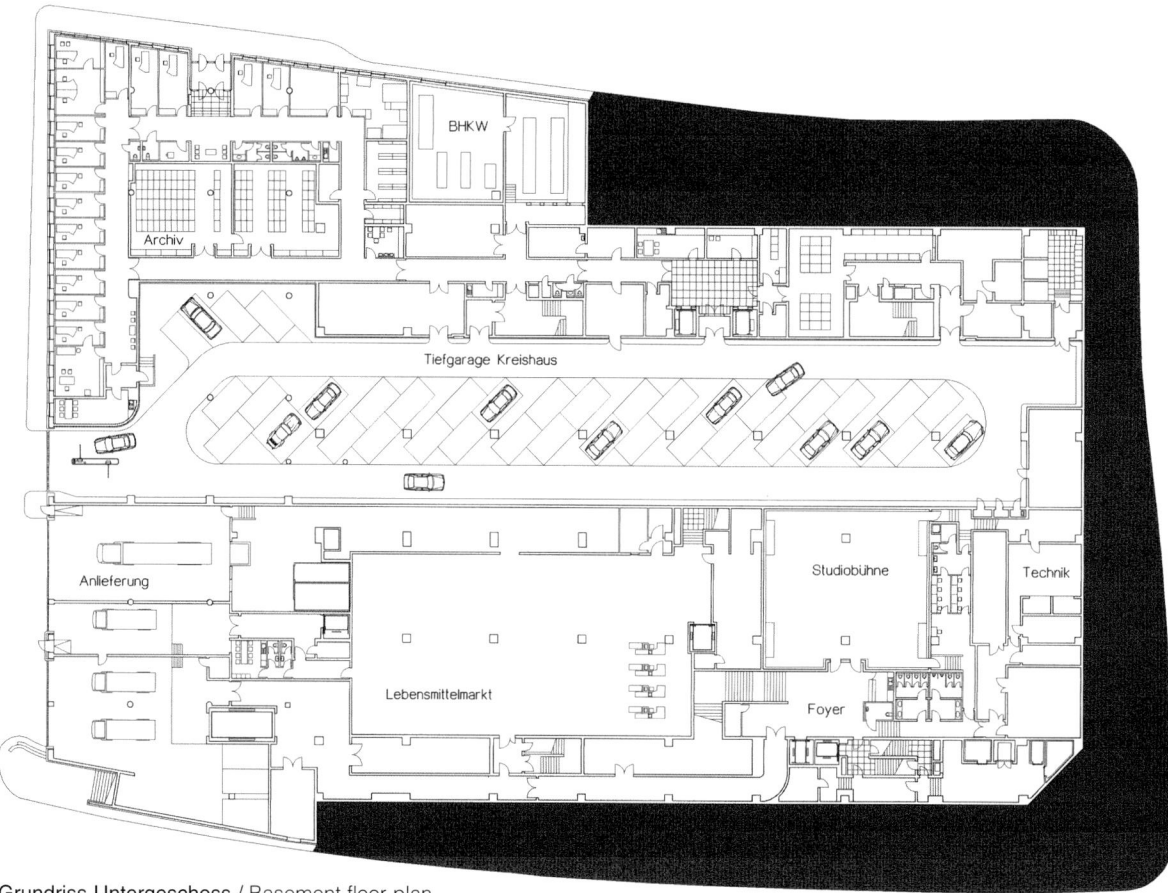

Grundriss Untergeschoss / Basement floor plan

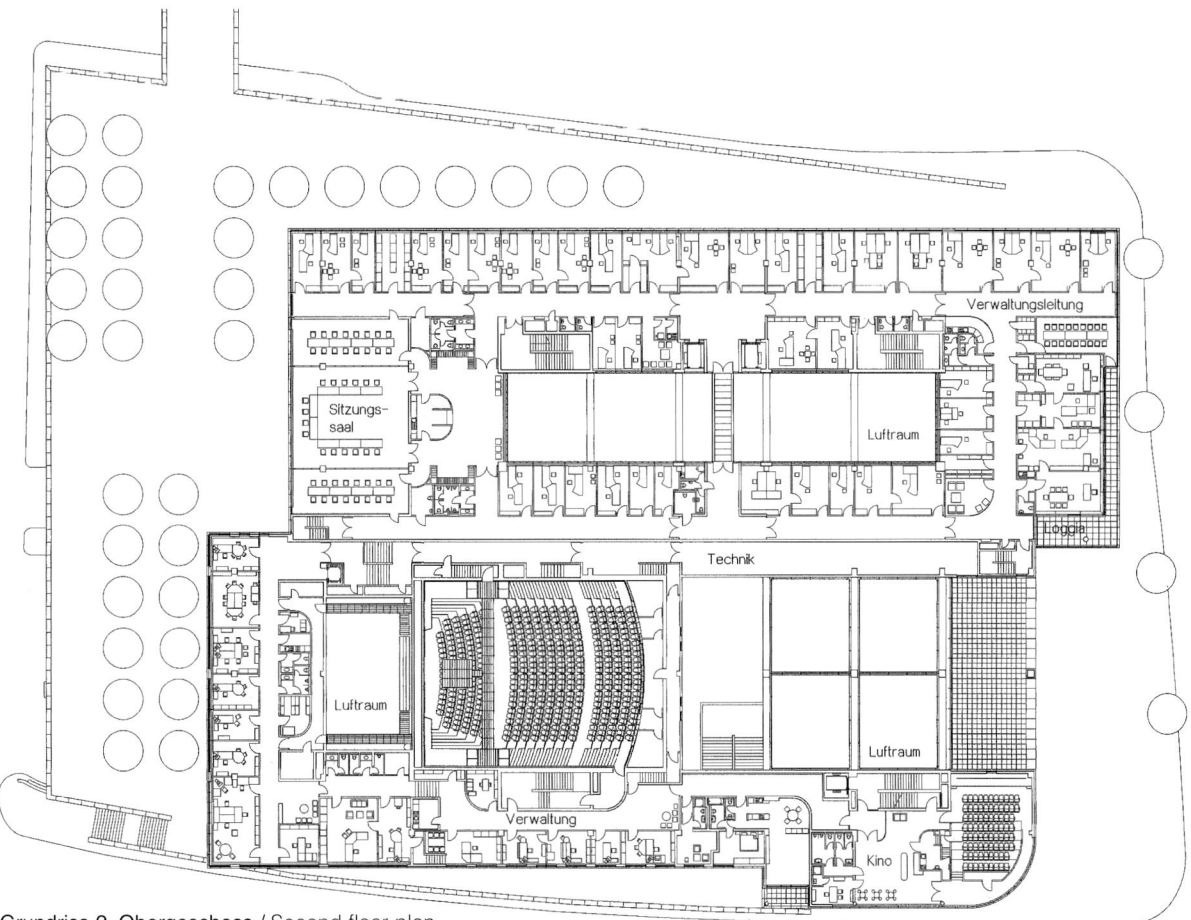

Grundriss 2. Obergeschoss / Second floor plan

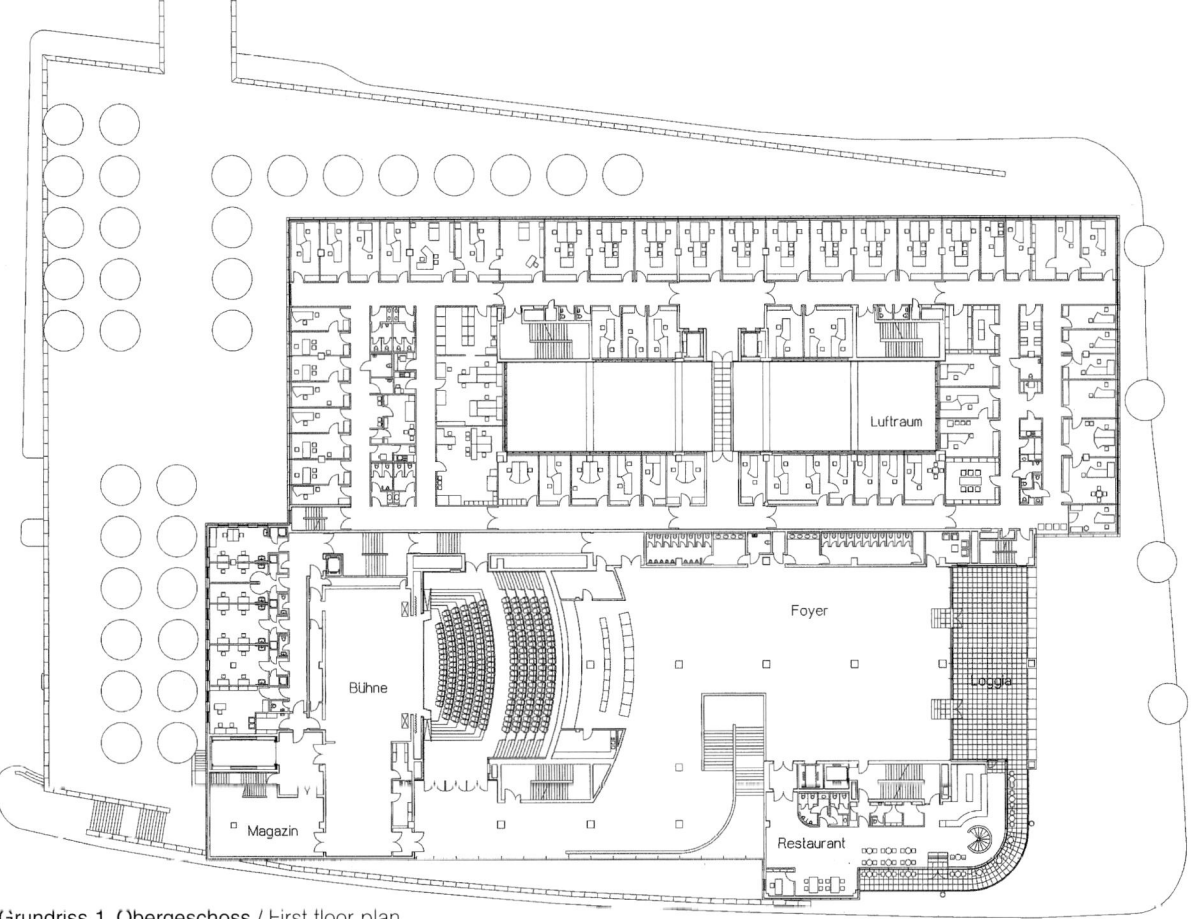

Grundriss 1. Obergeschoss / First floor plan

Projektdaten

Bauzeit	1998 – 2000	Foyer Schauspielhaus	960 m²
		Studiobühne	275 m²
Grundstücksfläche	8.643 m²	Sitzplätze Studiobühne	99
Überbaute Fläche	5.963 m²	Bühnenhaus	144 m²
Bruttogeschossfläche	22.850 m²	Bühnenhausmaße	L 16 m / B 9 m / H 15 m
Bruttorauminhalt	125.000 m³	Tranktor-Passage	375 m²
Gebäudehöhe	max. 22 m	Passagenlänge	70 m
Aussenmaße Kreishaus	33 x 89 m	Shops	1.900 m²
Bürofläche Kreishaus	4.000 m²	Shopanzahl	13
Lichthof Kreishaus	420 m²	Bar/Restaurant	300 m²
Lichthofmaße	L 46 m / B 9 m / H 17 m	Kino Hitch	250 m²
Aussenmaße Rheinisches Landestheater	34 x 89 m	Kinosaal	110 m²
Schauspielhaus	425 m²	Sitzplätze Kino	83
Sitzplätze Schauspielhaus	443		

Project data

Construction period	1998 – 2000	Theatre	425 m²
		No. of theatre seats	443
Site area	8,643 m²	Theatre foyer	960 m²
Footprint	5,963 m²	Studio theatre	275 m²
Gross floor area	22,850 m²	No. of seats in studio theatre	99
Gross volume	125,000 m³	Fly tower	144 m²
Height of building	max. 22 m	Fly tower dimensions	16 m x 9 m x 15 m high
External dimensions of district administration	33 x 89 m	Arcade	375 m²
		Length of arcade	70 m
Office floor area of district administration	4,000 m²	Shops	1,900 m²
		No. of shops	13
Atrium in district administration	420 m²	Bar/Restaurant	300 m²
Dimensions of atrium	46 m x 9 m x 17 m high	Hitch cinema	250 m²
External dimensions of Rheinisches Landestheater	34 x 89 m	Cinema auditorium	110 m²
		No. of cinema seats	83

| Projektbeteiligte | Persons and organizations involved in the project |

Bauherren

Kreishaus
Kreis Neuss, vertreten durch Kreishochbauamt Grevenbroich

Rheinisches Landestheater / Passage / Restaurant / Kino Hitch
Neusser Bauverein AG, Neuss

Inneneinrichtung Rheinisches Landestheater
Stadt Neuss, vertreten durch Kulturamt Neuss

Projektsteuerung
für das Kreishaus
Modernes Neuss Grundstücks und Bau GmbH, Neuss

Architekten
Ingenhoven & Ingenhoven, Neuss
Robert Ingenhoven, Oliver Ingenhoven

Mitarbeiter: Thomas Feinweber, Katrin Göritz, Markus Hüls, Norbert Keitlinghaus, Marion Roschmann

Objektüberwachung
Ingenhoven & Ingenhoven, Neuss
Ulrich Hochgürtel, Oberhausen

Tragwerksplanung
Ingenieur Büro AG Hubertus Zimmerling, Düsseldorf

Haustechnik HLSE
Wilmshöfer Beratende Ingenieure VBI, Düsseldorf

Bodengutachten
Ingenieurbüro Hans Siedek, Düsseldorf

Brandschutz
Ökotec Sachverständige, Schwalmtal

Bauphysik
Trümper, Overath, Heimann, Römer
Ingenieurgesellschaft für Bauphysik, Bergisch Gladbach

Prüfstatik
Gehlen Ingenieurbüro für Tragwerksplanung, Düsseldorf

Vermessung
Heinz Neuenhausen ÖbV, Neuss

Generalunternehmer
Dyckerhoff & Widmann AG, Niederlassung Düsseldorf

Fassade
Josef Gartner & Co. Nederland N.V., Heerlen

Bühnentechnik
Bühnenbau Schnakenberg GmbH & Co. KG, Wuppertal

Clients

District administration offices
District of Neuss, represented by Kreishochbauamt Grevenbroich

Theatre (RLT) / Arcade / Restaurant / Hitch cinema
Neusser Bauverein AG, Neuss

Furnishings theatre (RLT)
City of Neuss, represented by Kulturamt Neuss

Project management
for the district offices
Modernes Neuss Grundstücks und Bau GmbH, Neuss

Architects
Ingenhoven & Ingenhoven, Neuss
Robert Ingenhoven, Oliver Ingenhoven

Assistants: Thomas Feinweber, Katrin Göritz, Markus Hüls, Norbert Keitlinghaus, Marion Roschmann

Site supervision
Ingenhoven & Ingenhoven, Neuss
Ulrich Hochgürtel, Oberhausen

Structural engineers
Ingenieur Büro AG Hubertus Zimmerling, Düsseldorf

Mechanical services (heating, ventilation, sanitary and electrical installation)
Wilmshöfer Beratende Ingenieure VBI, Düsseldorf

Soil investigation
Ingenieurbüro Hans Siedek, Düsseldorf

Fire protection
Ökotec Sachverständige, Schwalmtal

Building physics
Trümper, Overath, Heimann, Römer

Control and analysis of structural calculations
Gehlen Ingenieurbüro für Tragswerkplanung, Düsseldorf

Surveying services
Heinz Neuenhausen ÖbV, Neuss

General contractor
Dyckerhoff & Widmann AG, Düsseldorf branch

Facade
Josef Gartner & Co., Heerlen, Netherlands

Stage mechanics
Bühnenbau Schnakenberg GmbH & Co. KG, Wuppertal

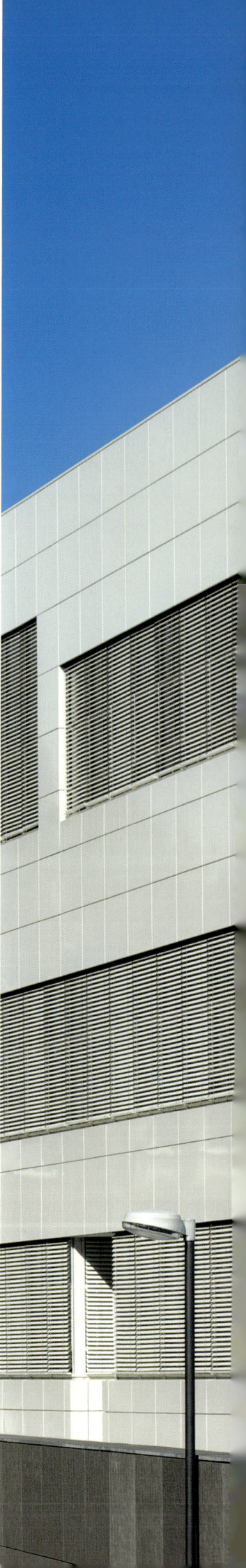

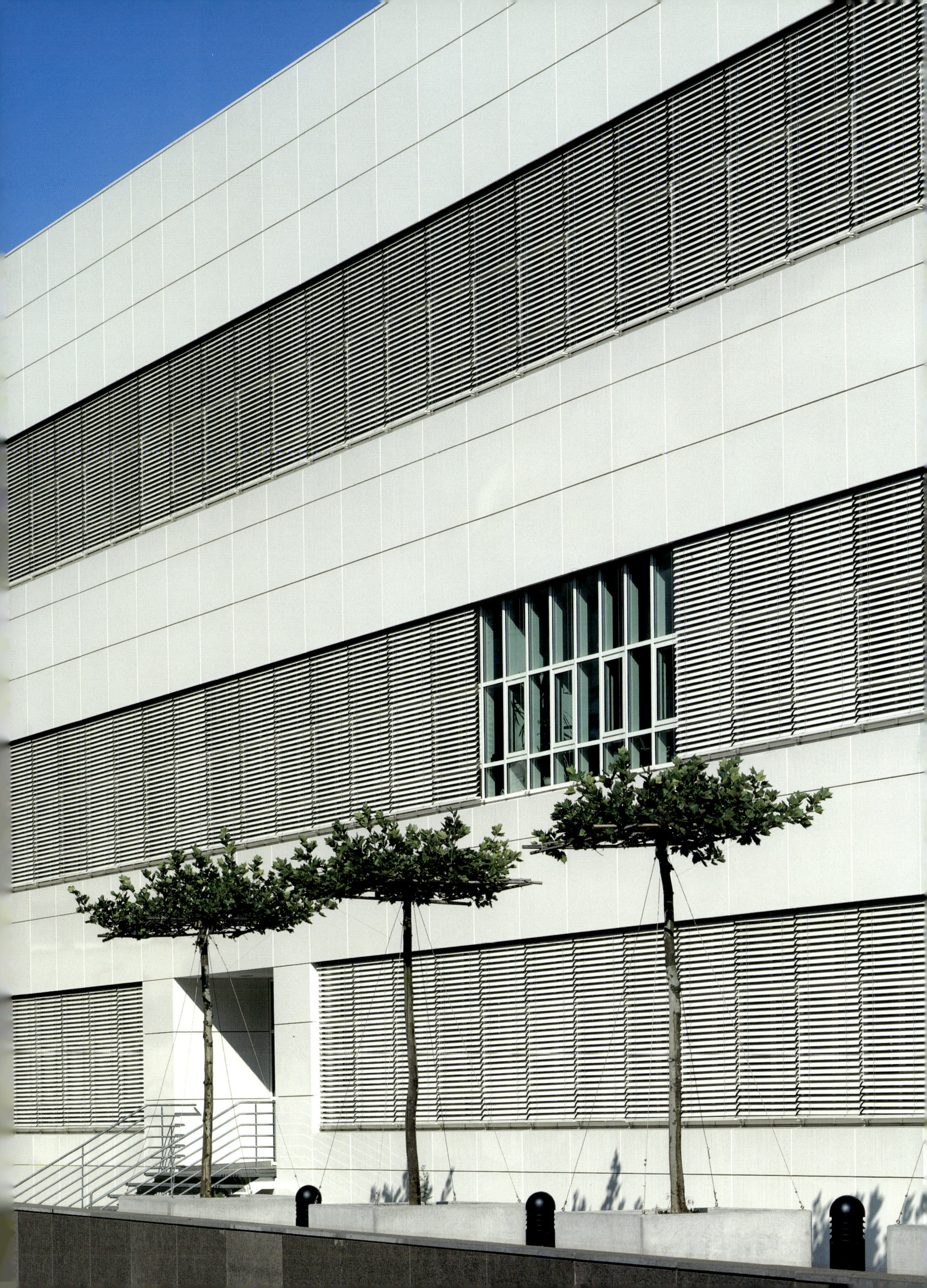

Ausgewählte Bauten und Projekte
Selected buildings and projects

Privathaus Neuss
1964 – 1965,
Holzbaupreis 1966

Private house, Neuss,
1964 – 65;
Timber Construction Prize,
1966

Büro- und Wohnhaus Neuss
1980 – 1982,
Anerkennung Deutscher
Architekturpreis 1983

Office and housing development, Neuss 1980 – 82;
German Architecture Prize
1983 (acknowledgement)

Autohaus Düsseldorf 1969 – 1972
Car salesrooms, Düsseldorf 1969 – 72

Sparkasse Neuss 1980 – 1982
Sparkasse Neuss 1980 – 82

Kupferpassage Coesfeld 1979 – 1984, BDA Architekturpreis 1985
Kupferpassage, Coesfeld 1979 – 84; BDA Architecture Prize, 1985

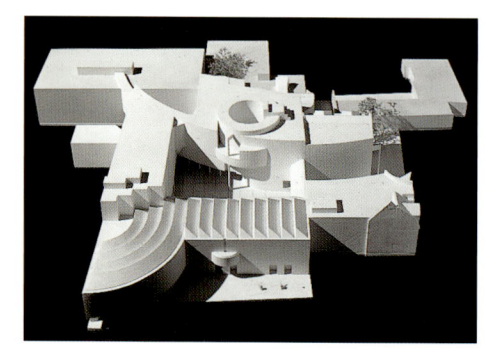

Germanisches Nationalmuseum Nürnberg 1984, Wettbewerb Ankauf
German National Museum, Nuremberg 1984; competition: purchase of scheme

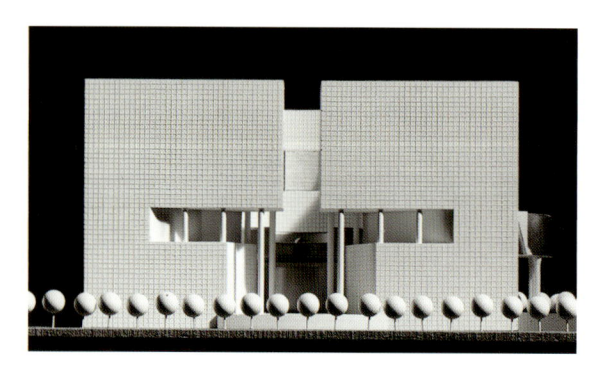

Landtag NRW Düsseldorf 1980, Wettbewerb
State parliament of North Rhine-Westphalia, Düsseldorf 1980;
competition

Einkaufszentrum
Castrop Rauxel
1986 – 1990,
Wettbewerb 1. Preis

Shopping centre,
Castrop Rauxel,
1986 – 90;
competition: first prize

Wohnbebauung am Rosengarten Neuss 1989 – 1991,
Wettbewerb 1. Preis
Housing development Am Rosengarten, Neuss 1989 – 91;
competition: first prize

Volksbank Rheine
1993 – 1994

Volksbank, Rheine
1993 – 94

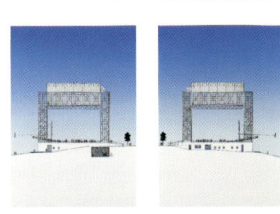

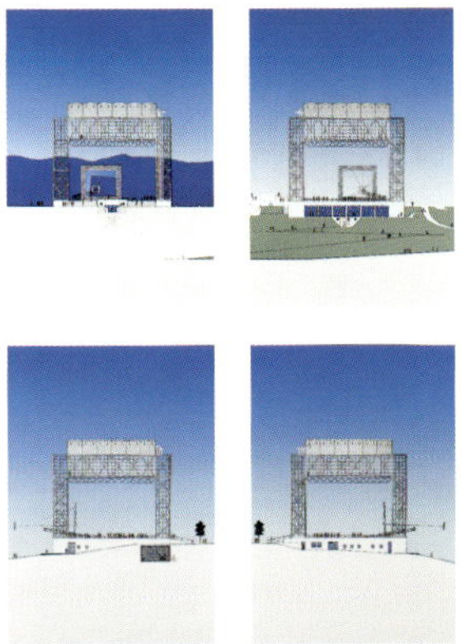

Documenta Ausstellungs-
halle Kassel 1989,
Wettbewerb Ankauf

Exhibition hall for
Documenta, Kassel 1989;
competition: purchase
of scheme

Warenhaus Frankfurt
1995

Department store, Frankfurt
1995

Privathaus Neuss 1992 – 1997
Private house, Neuss 1992 – 97

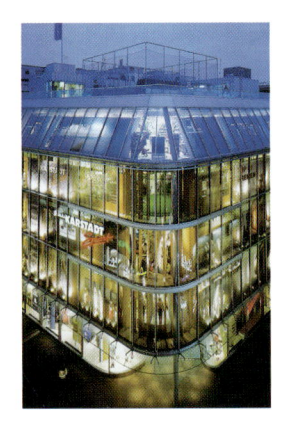

Sporthaus Bremen
1995 – 1997

Sports store, Bremen
1995 – 97

Sporthaus Düsseldorf 1992 – 1993
Sports store, Düsseldorf 1992 – 93

Museo del Prado Madrid 1995, Wettbewerb
Museo del Prado, Madrid 1995; competition

61

Warenhaus Konstanz 1996
Department store, Constance 1996

Privathaus Neuss 1999
Private house, Neuss 1999

Pfarrkirche St. Theodor Köln 1997, Wettbewerb
St Theodor's Church, Cologne 1997; competition

Wohn- und Geschäftshaus Neuss 1999
Housing and commercial development, Neuss 1999

Zentrum für Türkeistudien Essen 1997 – 1998
Centre for Turkish Studies, Essen 1997 – 98

Alte Post Rheine 1997, Wettbewerb 2. Preis
Alte Post, Rheine 1997; competition: second prize

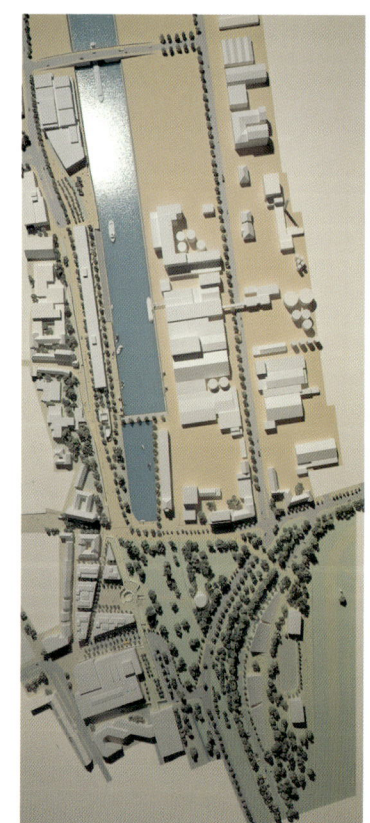

Hessentor Neuss
1999 – 2000,
Wettbewerb 1. Preis

Hessentor, Neuss
1999 – 2000;
competition: first prize

Josten am Hafen Neuss 2000, Wettbewerb 1. Preis
Josten am Hafen, Neuss 2000; competition: first prize

Umbau einer Lagerhalle im Hafen Neuss 2001
Harbour warehouse conversion, Neuss 2001

Privathaus 2000
Private house 2000

Seriell vorgefertigtes Holzhaus 2001
Prefabricated, standard-component timber house 2001

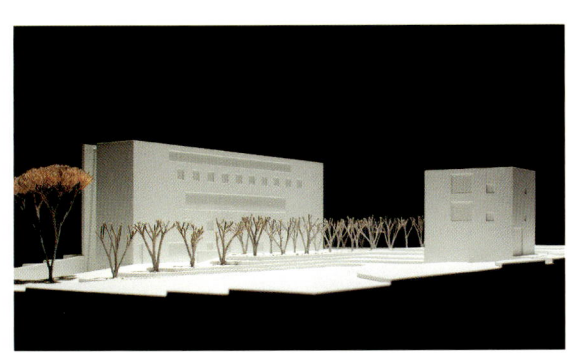

Museum für moderne Kunst Bozen 2001, Wettbewerb
Museum for Modern Art, Bolzano 2001; competition

Einfamilienhausbebauung Neuss 2001 – 2003
Single-family house, Neuss 2001 – 03

Bürohochhaus Neuss 2001
Office tower, Neuss 2001

Wohnhaus Neuss 2001 – 2003
House, Neuss 2001 – 03

Bebauung Busbahnhof
Neuss 2002 – 2004

Bus station development,
Neuss 2002 – 04

Impressum

Imprint

Fotografien / Photographs: © Studio Holger Knauf, Düsseldorf
(Hermann Fahlenbrach, Holger Knauf, Gunnar Nicolaus, Caroline
Pfeil) mit folgenden Ausnahmen / with the following exceptions:
Gaab & Stamminger, Düsseldorf: S. 62 rechts: zweites Foto
von oben / p. 62, right: second photo from top
Inge Goertz-Bauer, Düsseldorf: S. 60 links: viertes Foto
von oben / p. 60, left: fourth photo from top
Inken Kuntze, Düsseldorf: S. 61 rechts oben / p. 61: top right
Friedhelm Thomas, Lugano: S. 60 links: erstes und zweites
Foto von oben / p. 60, left: top two photos

© Prestel Verlag, München · Berlin · London · New York, 2002

Auf dem Umschlag / Cover: Rheinisches Landestheater, Neuss
Fotografie / Photograph: Studio Holger Knauf, Düsseldorf

Die Deutsche Bibliothek – CIP Einheitsaufnahme
Ein Titelsatz für diese Publikation ist bei der Deutschen Bibliothek
erhältlich

Library of Congress Control Number: 2002 103 189

Prestel Verlag · Mandlstraße 26 · 80802 München
Tel. +49 (0)89/381709-0 · Fax +49 (0)89/381709-35

www.prestel.de

4 Bloomsbury Place · London WC1A 2QA
Tel. +44 (0)20/7323-5004 · Fax +44 (0)20/7636-8004

175 5th Ave., Suite 402 · New York, NY 10010
Tel. +1 (212) 995-2720, Fax +1 (212) 995-2733

www.prestel.com

Translated from the German by Peter Green

Lektorat / Editor: Stella Sämann
Gestaltung und Herstellung / Design and Production:
Heinz Ross, München
Reproduktion / Lithography: ReproLine GmbH, München
Druck und Bindung / Printing and Binding:
Sellier Druck GmbH, Freising

Gedruckt auf chlorfrei gebleichtem Papier /
Printed on acid-free paper

Printed in Germany
ISBN 3-7913-2653-8